To: Dad
From: Adam
6/13/03

WAR IN THE PACIFIC

FROM THE FALL OF SINGAPORE TO JAPANESE SURRENDER

WAR IN THE PACIFIC

FROM THE FALL OF SINGAPORE TO JAPANESE SURRENDER

Jerry Scutts

THUNDER BAY
P·R·E·S·S

Published in the United States by
Thunder Bay Press
An imprint of the Advantage Publishers Group
5880 Oberlin Drive
San Diego, CA 92121-4794
www.advantagebooksonline.com

Produced by PRC Publishing Ltd
Kiln House, 210 New Kings Road
London SW6 4NZ

ISBN 1 57145 263 X

Library of Congress Cataloging-in-Publication Data available
upon request.

Printed and bound in China

1 2 3 4 5 00 01 02 03

The Photographs
The Public Record Office was the source of the bulk of the
photographs used in this book. Crown Copyright material in
the Public Record Office is reproduced by permission of the
Controller of Her Majesty's Stationery Office. Images are
reproduced courtesy of the Public Record Office.

Much of the illustrative material in this book was
photographed during active wartime missions. This
accounts for a lack of quality in some photographs, which
are reproduced for their rarity and interest rather than
their technical quality.

ABBREVIATIONS & GLOSSARY

AAA	Anti-aircraft artillery
ABDA	American, British, Dutch, Australian
Adm.	Admiral
AEAF	Allied Expeditionary Air Force
BG	Bomb Group (USAAF)
BPF	British Pacific Force
BS	Bomb Squadron (USAAF)
CAP	Combat air patrol
Capt	Captain
CBI	China-Burma-India (Theater)
C-i-C	Commander-in-chief
CIU	Central Interpretation Unit
CO	Commanding Officer
Col.	Colonel
cu in	cubic inch
DFC	Distinguished Flying Cross
DSO	Distinguished Service Order
ft	feet
Gen.	General
GOC	General officer commanding
HE	High explosive
IJN	Imperial Japanese Navy
in	inch
lb	pound
JAAF	Japanese Army Air Force
JNAF	Japanese Navy Air Force
LSM	Landing ship,
LST	Landind ship, tank
Lt-Col.	Lieutenant-colonel
Lt-Gen.	Lieutenant-general
Mk.	Mark
MT	Motor Transport
No.	Number
OSS	Office of Strategic Services (U.S.)
PA	Philippine Army
Para	Parachute
PFF	Path Finder Force
PoW	Prisoner of War
PIU	Photographic Interpretation Unit
PR	Photo-reconnaissance
PRS	PR Squadron
PRU	PR Unit
RAAF	Royal Australian Air Force
RAF	Royal Air Force
RCAF	Royal Canadian Air Force
RNAS	Royal Naval Air Service
RNZAF	Royal New Zealand Air Force
SAAF	South African Air Force
SEAC	Southeast Asia Command
SEATO	Southeast Asia Treaty Organization
Sgt	Sergeant
SOE	Special Operations Executive (British)
sq in	square inch
Sqn	Squadron (RAF)
TacR	Tactical reconnaissance
TAF	Tactical Air Force
TRG	Tactical Reconnaissance Group
TRS	Tactical Reconnaissance Squadron
USAAF/C	U.S. Army Air Force/Corps
USAFFE	U.S. Army Forces in the Far East
Vice-Adm.	Vice-Admiral

Note on Unit Nomenclature
Military units tend to have a preferred method of description
which is not always logical. In this book Allied armies are
spelled out (US First Army); corps are given Roman numerals
(XXXth Corps); divisions, regiments, squadrons, and units use
Arabic numerals (16th). RAF, RCAF, RAAF, and SAAF
squadrons are identified by their number (No 617).

CONTENTS

INTRODUCTION

Japan's war with China in the last half of the 1930s offered numerous dangerous pointers to any Western observer in a position to evaluate them—unprecedentedly long-range bombing raids, the ruthless terror thus unleashed on "open" cities without warning, and the harshness with which the Japanese Imperial Army dealt with prisoners of war and civilians alike clearly demonstrated that here was a nation to be reckoned with. Very little of this clear evidence of Japanese military prowess was heeded by Western nations, and although some aid was given to the Chinese, substantial areas of the country fell under foreign rule.

A nation beset with widespread unrest and unemployment, Japan in the 1920s and 30s was ripe for a new order and strong leadership. As the country gradually fell under the influence of militaristic elements, Emperor Hirohito generally acquiesced to their rising power. These self-styled warlords swayed the people by their propaganda and increasingly rejected Western influence and further erosion of Japan's ancient traditions. They vowed to restore the country's international prestige and ultimately to remove the influence that foreign colonial power had imposed on Asia for decades. Dominion and exploitation by Europeans, be they British, French or Dutch, was seen as an evil that Japan took upon herself to terminate forever.

Japan's war in China

Japan began military operations against Manchuria on September 10, 1931, when troops of the Kwantung Army guarding the Manchurian railways began fighting the Chinese at Mukden, an action taken on the slim pretext that China was about to attack the Japanese. In vain China protested and appealed strongly to the League of Nations. Japanese troops remained in place while their government planned further incursions aimed at securing large areas of mainland China, by force if necessary.

Chiang Kai-shek was elected president of the Chinese executive on December 1, 1935. The following year the military faction in Japan appointed Hirota prime minister. A staged kidnapping of the Chinese nationalist leader (the

Below: Japanese troops preparing to assault an enemy position early in the country's 14-year war with neighboring China. Masters of traversing natural obstacles, the Imperial troops appear to have used pontoon boats to cross a waterway.

Sian Incident) forced Chiang to declare war on Japan on December 12, 1936, although open hostilities between the two nations did not begin officially until the clash at the Marco Polo railway bridge near Peking on July 7, 1937. This incident marked the recognized start of the Sino-Japanese war—which Japan insisted on playing down and referring to merely as the "China Incident."

In Japan, on July 1, Prince Konoye had become prime minister with Hirota foreign

Above: During operations in Shanghai early in 1932 Japanese naval troops established rallying points for landing parties—such as this one in the Chapei area.

Below: Indiscriminate Japanese bombing raids caused widespread damage and civilian casualties in many Chinese provinces. A road-rail crossing at Jukong was the scene of a typical raid in 1932.

Right: Japanese engineers take up firing positions for the camera during a rifle drill exercise in China.

Below: Smoke rises from stricken U.S. warships after the attack on Pearl Harbor.

Above: A vertical photograph of Battleship Row, Peal Harbor after the Japanese attack. Oil seeps from the shattered *Arizona*, worst casualty of the attack in human terms.

minister. Imperial troops seized Peking by July 28. Having previously aligned the country with Germany by the Anti-Comintern Pact of November 25, 1936, Japan's intentions were clear enough. Events in China brought adverse reaction from America but, again, little was actually done to help Chiang Kai-shek's desperate struggle to repel the Japanese. Woefully ill-equipped to fight a modern war, the nationalist government's appeals to the League of Nations continued to fall on deaf ears.

China's spirit was hard to crush, however, and international indifference to her plight did not prevent resistance to the invader. Japan's battle casualties began to mount even though her losses were usually less than those of her adversaries. With huge reserves of manpower at their disposal, Chinese forces could afford to take casualties in tenacious defensive actions in which they refused to surrender ground cheaply.

Condemnation of Japan's actions in China failed to stir the West until successively brutal acts of repression—particularly the infamous "Rape of Nanking" on December 12–13, 1937, gradually hardened attitudes. A puppet government, wholly subservient to the Japanese, was set up in Nanking on March 28, 1938, and for China, the war continued to bring one disaster after another. For her part Japan may have subjugated large areas of China—including the capital—but Russia remained a potential threat; had Stalin so chosen, his armies could have made life extremely difficult for the invaders of China. Notwithstanding incidents such as that on July 11, 1938, when Russian troops clashed with the Japanese on the border of Manchukuo—Manchuria under a new name imposed on the Chinese and recognized by Germany on May 12—no large-scale Soviet involvement occurred. War with Russia was avoided even after another border clash in Manchukuo in August 1939 when 11,000 Japanese troops were killed.

Japan remained wary of her powerful neighbor, even after the Soviet Union signed a non-aggression pact with Hitler's Germany in August 1939—a signing which, on the face of it, placed Prince Konoye's government and the USSR on the same Axis side. Differences between the two nations were formally settled on April 13, 1941, with the signing of a Japanese-Soviet Neutrality Pact.

Japan's military actions continued to lose her support in the West, and by the time Franklin Roosevelt won a third term as U.S. president in November 1940, adverse reaction to the Sino-Japanese war had changed the way many Americans perceived the outside world. Isolationism gradually lost ground as Roosevelt's Democrats sought ways to assist friendly nations materially without actually going to war.

When World War II began in Europe in September 1939, Japan's intention to create what was grandly named the Greater Southeast Asian Co-Prosperity Sphere came nearer realization. Germany's early subjugation of France and the Netherlands removed the power base of two of the major colonial powers in Asia. If Japan could contain China—a task of such magnitude that even the ambitious warlords did not minimize it—then the promised prosperity could flourish. What the Japanese did not state publicly was that this prosperity would come about by force of arms and serve Nipponese interests almost exclusively from a position created by military domination of the "partners" who—willingly or not—would be brought into the sphere of influence.

In trying to exert pressure on the United States and Britain to recognize her superior position in the East, Japan came up against deepening hostility and economic sanctions. The U.S. made a complete troop withdrawal from China conditional on any such recognition of the country. It was no surprise that Japan rejected this demand, despite the fact that conducting military operations in China and stationing troops and air units there were costing her dearly.

China's resources became vital to Japan, which soon looked further afield for sources of

Above: Revving up on the deck of one of Nagumo's carriers, Mitsubishi A6M Zero-sen fighters prepare to attack Pearl Harbor on December 7, 1941.

Right: Allied photo-reconnaissance capability in the Pacific was greatly expanded to include photoflash night photography, this vertical highlighting a bridge.

commodities, particularly oil and rubber. Japanese troops landed in Indo-China on July 28, 1940, following an agreement by the French Vichy government that bases in that country could be used. Three days before it was announced that Japanese assets would be frozen by the United States and Britain and her Dominions. Japan took reciprocal action, and on the 29th, her aircraft bombed a U.S. gunboat at Chunking.

Trade embargoes by the West pushed an intransigent Japan to the limit of economic endurance and the militarist government took an irrevocable decision to go to war, to take what the country needed by force. As a curtain raiser, they would carry out surprise attacks on American and British bases across the Pacific. Spearheaded by the Fast Carrier Striking Force under the able command of Vice-Adm. Chuichi Nagumo, the Japanese had every confidence in

11

CENERAL EXPLANATION.

THIS PHOTO-DIAGRAM EXPLAINS THE CORRECT CAMERA OPERATION WHEN THE DAY TYPE T.35 CONTROL IS USED.

THE SYSTEM OF PHOTOGRAPHY IS THE 'OPEN PLATE' METHOD, WHEREBY A FRAME OF THE FILM IS ALWAYS UNDER EXPOSURE IN THE CAMERA. THE SHUTTER FUNCTIONS MERELY FOR THE PURPOSE OF ALLOWING THE FILM TO BE WOUND OVER. THUS EXPOSURES MADE ARE SUBJECT TO THE PHOTOFLASH WHICH ILLUMIN-ATES GROUND DETAIL AND IS INTENDED TO COINCIDE WITH THE BOMB BURSTS. THE MUZZLE FLAMES OF GUNS, FIRES, SEARCH-LIGHTS, DECOY LIGHTS AND LIGHTING SYSTEMS WILL BE AUTOMATICALLY RECORDED BY THE FRAME OF THE FILM UNDER EXPOSURE AT THE TIME.

ON THE RIGHT ARE 3 ILLUSTRATIONS SHOW-ING TYPICAL EXTRACTS FROM NIGHT FILMS WITH ARROWS INDICATING THE FRAME OR FRAMES OF THE FILM ON WHICH THEY WOULD BE EXPECTED TO BE FOUND.

IT WILL BE SEEN THAT INFORMATION OF MUCH VALUE IS RECORDED ON FRAMES OTHER THAN THAT SHOWING GROUND DETAIL. IT IS MOST IMPORTANT FOR THIS REASON TO OPERATE THE CAMERA BOTH BEFORE AND AFTER BOMBING AS INDICATED.

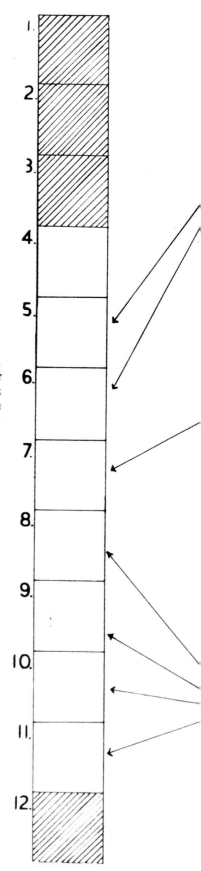

THESE TWO FRAMES OF THE FILM ARE WOUND OVER ON THE GROUND AND WILL BE FOGGED BY LIGHT.

THIS FRAME IS UNDER EXPOSURE ON THE JOURNEY TO THE TARGET AND WILL BE FOGGED BY LIGHT.

IMMEDIATELY BEFORE THE TARGET AREA IS REACHED THE BUTTON ON THE T.35 CONTROL IS PRESSED TWICE. THIS WINDS THE FILM OVER TO FRAME NO. 4 AND THEN ON TO FRAME NO. 5. WITH FRAME NO. 5 IN POSITION THE BOMBS ARE RELEASED AND THE T.35 CONTROL IS SWITCHED ON.

ACCORDING TO THE HEIGHT OF THE AIRCRAFT, APPROXIMATELY 5 TO 10 SECONDS AFTER THE BOMBS HAVE BEEN RELEASED, THE FLASH IS LAUNCHED. THE CONTROL WILL HAVE WOUND FRAME NO. 6 INTO POSITION BY THIS TIME.

THE CONTROL THEN WINDS FRAME NO. 7 INTO POSITION AND THE FLASH EXPLODES ILLUMIN-ATING THE BOMB BURSTS.

THE OPERATOR THEN PRESSES THE BUTTON ON THE T.35 CONTROL ON SEEING THE FLASH EXPLODE AND THIS BRINGS FRAME NO. 8 INTO POSITION. THE CONTROL IS THEN SWITCHED OFF.

ON LEAVING THE TARGET AREA THE BUTTON ON THE T.35 CONTROL IS PRESSED THREE TIMES, WITH A SHORT INTERVAL BETWEEN EACH OPERATION.

THIS BRINGS FRAME NO. 9 AND THEN FRAME NO. 10 INTO POSITION FOR SHORT PERIODS. FRAME NO. 11 IS BROUGHT INTO POSITION BY THE THIRD OPERATION OF THE BUTTON.

AS THE TARGET AREA IS LEFT BEHIND THE BUTTON IS PRESSED ONCE MORE AND FRAME NO. 12 IS BROUGHT UNDER EXPOSURE. THIS FRAME WILL FOG UP ON THE WAY TO BASE UNLESS OF COURSE FURTHER PICTURES ARE ATTEMPTED.

RAPHY.
RESULTS

SECRET

A TYPICAL RECORDING ON A FRAME NO. 5
OR NO. 6.
IT SHOWS TWO GUNS FIRING FROM A L.A.
BATTERY. THE MUZZLE FLAMES FROM THE
GUNS HAVE ILLUMINATED SURROUNDING
GROUND DETAIL AND MADE IT POSSIBLE TO
FIND THE LOCATION OF THE BATTERY.
A RECORDING OF THIS NATURE MIGHT
EQUALLY WELL HAVE OCCURRED, OF COURSE
ON FRAMES NOS. 8 - 11.

A PHOTOGRAPH RECORDED ON THE FILM WHEN
THE PHOTOFLASH EXPLODED TO ILLUMINATE
THE BOMB BURSTS. THE BOMB FLASHES ARE
SEEN IMMEDIATELY BELOW THE BURSTS.

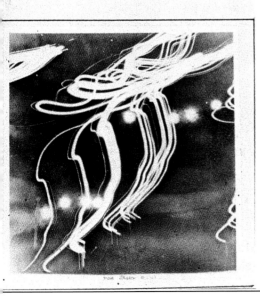

HERE IS THE FRAME OF A FILM WHICH FOLLOWED
THE ACTUAL PHOTOGRAPH. NOTE THE TWO
GROUPS OF FIRE TRACES. THE POINTS
RESEMBLANCE OF THESE TRACES INDICATE
DISTANCE BETWEEN, AND THE LAYOUT OF
FIRES, WHILE THE SIZE OR BREADTH OF THE
TRACES GIVES AN INDICATION OF THE SIZE OF
THE FIRES. THE GUNS OF A 4-GUN BATTERY
ARE SEEN FIRING TWICE. SUCH A FLAME
MIGHT BE EXPECTED ON FRAMES NOS. 8 TO 11,
OR, FOR THAT MATTER, ON NUMBERS 5 OR 6.

P.I.D.B./C 934 B. 13 : 7 : 43.

Left: A classified wartime guide to night photography using the Type T35 control to obtain sequential exposures during target runs.

The technique, given in the general explanation, used the 'open frame' method, whereby a frame of film was always under exposure in the camera. The shutter functioned merely for the purpose of allowing film to wind on, so that the exposures took place when the photoflash illuminated the target, intended to coincide with the bomb bursts. The photograph would also show muzzle flashes from guns, searchlight beams, fires, decoy lights and other lighting systems. On the right, example frames show typical extracts from night film and the arrows show where they could be expected to fall on the film.

The diagrammatic representation of the film shows: the first two frames of film fogged over because they were exposed on the ground; a third frame fogged over because it was exposed on the journey to the target. Immediately before the target was reached the T.35 control was pressed twice, winding the film to frame 5 which was exposed when the bombs were released. Five to ten seconds later frame 6 was exposed once the flash was launched, and frame 7 caught the bomb bursts. The operator pressed the control again on seeing the flash and this wound on to frame 8. On leaving the target area, three more exposures were taken and, finally, once the target area was left, the film wound on to frame 12 which would be fogged over on the journey home.

The photos at right show: top a typical frame 5 or 6 exposure showing gun muzzle flashes; the photoflash-illuminated frame 7; post-bomb burst photograph from frames 8 to 11 showing ground fire traces.

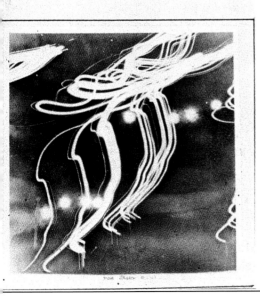

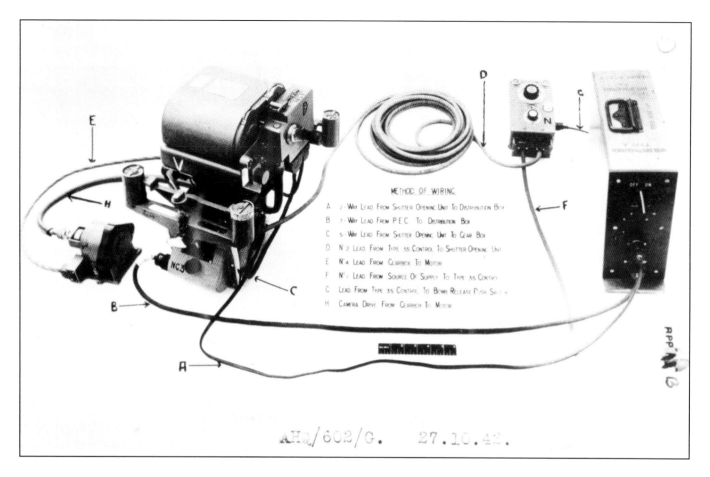

METHOD OF WIRING

A 2-Way Lead From Shutter Opening Unit To Distribution Box
B 7-Way Lead From P.E.C. To Distribution Box
C 5-Way Lead From Shutter Opening Unit To Gear Box
D No 2 Lead From Type 35 Control To Shutter Opening Unit
E No 4 Lead From Gearbox To Motor
F No 1 Lead From Source Of Supply To Type 35 Control
G Lead From Type 35 Control To Bomb Release Push Switch
H Camera Drive From Gearbox To Motor

AHQ/602/G.   27.10.42.

Above: Schematic wiring instructions to sychronize an aerial camera drive with an aircraft bomb release.

Below: Various accessories could be used to enhance and ensure continual and clear photo coverage. Superb clarity of image was widely achieved by Allied PR aircraft, often under difficult conditions.

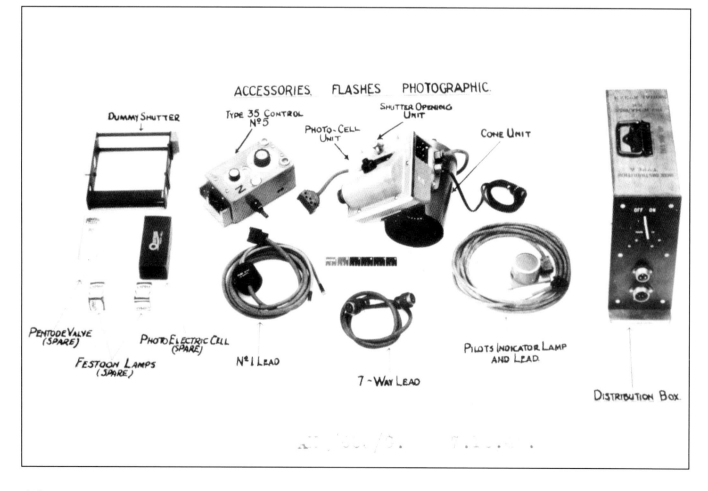

ACCESSORIES. FLASHES PHOTOGRAPHIC.

DUMMY SHUTTER

TYPE 35 CONTROL No 5

PHOTO-CELL UNIT

SHUTTER OPENING UNIT

CONE UNIT

PENTODE VALVE (SPARE)

PHOTO ELECTRIC CELL (SPARE)

FESTOON LAMPS (SPARE)

No 1 LEAD

7-WAY LEAD

PILOTS INDICATOR LAMP AND LEAD

DISTRIBUTION BOX

Above: The ever-useful amphtrac coping with the compacted volcanic ash of Iwo Jima.

Left: Operation "Ironclad" stopped Japanese annexation of Madagascar at a small cost to British forces from Vichy French units. Martlets of 881 Squadron shot down this MS406 of Esc de Chasse 565 on May 7, 1942.

an easy victory. Such a move had been planned by Admiral Isoroku Yamamoto who, although generally against making war on the United States, bowed to the inevitable. The decision to open hostilities was decided at an Imperial conference on September 6, and later that month preparations were made to begin "Southern Area" operations. War orders were issued to the Japanese armed forces on November 5, and on the 26th, Nagumo's carriers put to sea—destination Pearl Harbor.

As the carriers *Akagi*, *Kaga*, *Hiryu*, *Shokaku*, *Soryu* and *Zuikaku* launched their devastating strike on the U.S. Pacific Fleet in Pearl Harbor on December 7, 1941, the Japanese Army attacked the Philippines and Malaya. Although they faced numerically stronger adversaries, the Japanese gambled that the element of surprise would be very much in their favor and serve to fatally dilute the defensive effort and concentration the Western Allies could achieve. A not insubstantial factor was the sheer size of the land and sea area over which the Japanese intended to make war.

Strengths

Although such figures are invariably open to qualification and correction, the following statistics of Japanese army, navy, and air force strengths relative to those of the Allies serve, perhaps, to highlight the magnitude of the early victories. On the ground, the Imperial Army often outnumbered its enemies in the set-piece battles of the Pacific war but, in terms of firepower, it gradually lost ground. Imperial troops, imbued with the strict code of Bushido, often indulged in suicidal charges reminiscent of World War I, which served to whittle down the numbers of available troops.

On her entry into war Japan had 1,700,000 men under arms, a figure that gradually rose to reach 7,200,000 at the end of hostilities in 1945, to reflect the extent of mobilization.

As regards relative air strengths, in January 1942 Japanese front-line combat aircraft (combined Navy and Army) totals were 2,520 compared to 3,547 U.S. (combined Army Air Force, Navy, and Marines). In developing a number of technically world class combat aircraft, the Japanese policy of paying scant regard to protection of the crew, engines, and other vital areas caused enormous losses. Many of these would have survived air combat had a degree of protection been incorporated—as it ultimately was, but only after many front-line units had been decimated and irreplaceable pilots lost.

Japan's early war naval strength was impressive: the Imperial Japanese Navy (IJN) began war operations with 10 carriers, 10 battleships, 36 cruisers, 113 destroyers, and 63 submarines. Embarked aboard the fleet carriers were Mitsubishi A6M fighters, Aichi D3A "Val" dive bombers, and B2N "Kate" torpedo bombers— all the equals, if not the superiors, of contemporary foreign aircraft.

Left: Men scramble to get clear of further explosions in the aircraft deck park aboard the carrier *Bunker Hill* following a kamikaze strike.

Below: U.S. troops on Tinian in the Marianas during late 1944.

The IJN had begun the war with two outstanding weapons, the "Long Lance" torpedo and the Mitsubishi A6M Zero-sen (codenamed "Zeke") fighter. By bestowing an unprecedented 1,000 miles' range on the early versions of the "Zeke," Imperial Navy pilots appeared where single-engined fighters were totally unexpected; the adverse effect on Allied morale was immediate and predictable. Pitted against a motley collection of obsolete Allied aircraft, the Japanese quickly gained air superiority.

An armory of effective IJN naval weapons included the Type 91 aerial torpedo, a 17.7-inch weapon fitted with a wooden "air tail" which improved the angle at which it entered the water and prevented it diving too deeply. The tail broke off shortly after running depth was achieved. The Type 95 "Long Lance," an oxygen-driven, wakeless torpedo capable of running at a speed of 36–50 knots for 21,880 yards, was the best of its kind in service anywhere in the Pacific in the early war years. This was the standard torpedo aboard IJN cruisers and destroyers.

In terms of tanks, Japan built more than 2,500 examples of three light to medium classes, these seeing service from 1935. Tanks, although quite widely used during the Pacific war, were not the decisive weapons they were in other theaters. Japanese army artillery comprised guns of seven different designs ranging in caliber from 37mm to 240mm.

On the Allied side the most effective force in being was, undoubtedly, the aircraft carriers available to the U.S. Navy. Having avoided the destruction at Pearl Harbor, the U.S. Pacific Fleet carriers—each with their F4F Wildcat fighters, SBD Dauntless dive bombers, and TBD Devastator torpedo bombers—were a force to be reckoned with, a fact not lost on the Japanese.

Also with three carriers in the Far East, the Royal Navy suffered from still embarking obsolete aircraft such as the Swordfish, although there were some Fulmars and Sea Hurricane fighters. Events were to prove that the enemy was quite capable of removing any capital ship from the scene without difficulty. Having neutralized the American big-gun ships and sunk the two British battleships belatedly sent to meet the emergency, Japan dominated the seas in this respect for the first few vital months of the war.

Air superiority

In terms of fighter aircraft the most numerous, if not totally effective, were the American Curtiss

Above Left: Before SEAC embarked on recapturing Burma, extensive aerial photography of the country's transportation system was undertaken. A bridge at Pegu is clearly revealed in this view.

Top: U.S. troops going ashore on Leyte during late 1944.

Above: American amphibious DUKWs in a native village on Okinawa.

Above: The busy beachhead on Okinawa with LSTs unloading trucks, oil drums, Jeeps, and stores.

Above Left: A 1,000lb bomb about to add to the inferno that USS *San Jacinto*'s air group has already made of installations on Izumi airfield on Kyushu, Japan, March 18, 1945.

Left: Japanese coastal freighter under attack in late 1943.

P-40 Warhawk, Bell P-39 Airacobra, and Lockheed P-38 Lightning, although there were precious few of the latter until mass production really got underway. The RAF did what it could with a handful of Hawker Hurricanes, the most modern type available to its squadrons in the Far East, otherwise Brewster Buffaloes and a miscellany of obsolete types had to cope as best they could. RAF striking power was invested in antiquated Vickers Wildebeest biplane torpedo bombers, although Blenheims and Hudsons helped to redress the balance slightly.

The Dutch were equally hampered by aircraft such as the 1937-vintage Martin 139 bomber and Curtiss-Wright CW-21 fighter which, though efficient enough in their day, simply could not match the advances made by the Japanese in the years immediately prior to the

war. All Allied types were generally inferior to the Mitsubishi A6M on a straight comparison. That did not prevent some Allied success in air combat, which always relied on factors such as early warning, height advantage, numbers, and, above all, the relative skills of the opposing pilots.

The Japanese Army Air Force operated the capable Nakajima Ki-43 Hayabusa ("Oscar"), and while both of the air arms were equipped with excellent bombers, these were dangerously prone to destruction by fire. Fortunately for the Japanese many critical early war bombing missions were carried out without the Allies being able to take advantage of these deficiencies.

With the roll call of disaster that the events of December 1941 represented for the Allies, there was a vital need to fill the gap caused by lack of warning of Japanese intentions. Having an administrative infrastructure already in place in India, the British gained some breathing space after the retreats from Burma and Malaya, but little could be done in terms of offensive action until decimated forces could be rebuilt. Similarly, an American regional HQ was established in Australia with forward air bases in New Guinea. Dutch survivors of the debacle in Java were also able to regroup in Australia.

Reconnaissance rejuvenation

Aerial photography of Southeast Asia had been carried out to some extent before the war, but at the commencement of hostilities the exact disposition of Japanese air, land, and sea forces often became a matter of guesswork to Allied forces. During 1941–42 some of the most useful reconnaissance sorties were performed by RAAF Lockheed Hudsons. Fitted with makeshift camera equipment, these machines made a useful early contribution to intelligence data. An embryo PR organization was started in the Far East with two RAF Brewster Buffaloes. Flying with No. 4 Photographic Reconnaissance Unit (PRU), these machines performed valuable service during the Japanese invasion of Malaya. Hurricanes flew similar sorties in Burma.

Subsequently, No. 5 PRU was formed, initially operating five loaned B-25 Mitchells delivered to Australia under a pre-war Dutch order before Java fell. These aircraft were extensively used in the PR role until complemented, then supplanted, by Hurricanes and Spitfires in 1942–43. Mosquitos came with further expansion, and by the time the Allies went onto the offensive, No. 171 PR Wing had been formed. In its turn this unit became the Photographic Reconnaissance Force in February 1944, an amalgam of RAF and USAAF PR squadrons in Southeast Asia.

As the war progressed, numerous USAAF aircraft types—including the F-7 version of the B-24 and F-5 version of the P-38—flew PR sorties. In addition, there were photo-recon variants of all the U.S. Navy shipboard aircraft, plus land-based patrol bombers and flying boats combined to provide ample visual coverage of enemy targets.

It was ironic that the Japanese Army developed what was widely acknowledged as one of the best PR aircraft of the war, the Mitsubishi Ki-46. Superbly streamlined and very fast, the "Dinah" proved that, irrespective of quality and quantity, intelligence material is only of value when it can be turned to practical gain. For the Japanese, their reconnaissance efforts often led to no gain whatsoever.

Left: Marine PBJ-1 Mitchells en route to raid Rabaul in 1943.

DAY OF IGNOMINY

1. THE CAPTURE OF MALAYA AND FALL OF SINGAPORE

BACKGROUND

The early weeks of the Pacific war went better for the Japanese than they could ever have hoped. By crippling the U.S. fleet at Pearl Harbor and simultaneously invading Thailand and Malaya, landing troops on Guam and Wake Islands, and bombing Singapore and targets in the Philippines within the first 48 hours, they spread panic and confusion. The fact that the defense of these territories was vested largely in British and Commonwealth, U.S., and Dutch forces, which represented a loosely defined, poorly integrated, and multi-layered command structure, would prove more of an asset to the Japanese than the defenders.

A miscellany of Allied weapons, many of them obsolete, also failed to deter the invaders, few of whom could have predicted such a scale of gain in so short a time. The result for the Allies, as the Japanese Army advanced on all its chosen fronts, making the maximum use of the element of surprise, was the steady loss of war equipment and, eventually, thousands of troops, killed, wounded or captured.

For Britain, the disastrous turn of events in the Far East in late 1941 was almost beyond belief for a country that had then been at war for almost two years. Even if the nature of war with the European Axis powers was far from directly comparable to the conditions prevailing in Asia, the basic military requirements of modern weapons, sound intelligence, good communications, strong inter-service co-operation, unsullied by the folly of underestimating the enemy, should surely have been learned.

Events, however, were to prove these points had not been learned by a nation that was dangerously complacent and felt that, in this part of the world at least, the mere presence of Western military forces was more than enough of a deterrent to any Oriental army. For decades a Far Eastern posting had been regarded as sojourn in a peaceful backwater.

Below: During their advance through Malaya and Burma the Japanese showed their mastery in crossing any natural obstacle, including rivers using lightweight assault boats.

Top: Masters of infiltration, the Japanese moved quickly and effectively through difficult terrain and proved more than a match for the complacent colonial powers.

Above: The calm before the storm. Singapore in 1938 was a picture of tranquil British power, the garrison enjoying regular visits by the Royal Navy such as the destroyer seen here.

Amphibious landings by the Japanese brought about hurried, often ineffectual retaliation; the situation led to confused reports of enemy ships in a given area and missed sightings when the vessels rapidly changed course to land troops at an unexpected point. Equally frustrating were sightings of enemy activity where none had actually occurred. Some confirmation of all too obvious Japanese movement at sea could only be fragmentary due to overcast weather conditions and the ease at which vessels could be lost to sight. Far East time zone differences resulted in events occurring simultaneously though locally they were actually several hours apart.

THE INVASION OF MALAYA

Having left the port of Hainan on December 4, 1941, 18 transports had set course for Malaya carrying 26,640 troops of the 5th Infantry Division under Lt-Gen. Matsui, plus the 56th Infantry Regiment of the 18th Infantry Division. With a strong cruiser and destroyer screen, this task group was later joined by other warships—including submarines—and, on the 5th, by the Southern Expeditionary Force which had sailed from Saigon. This force included three transports carrying part of the 55th Division's 143rd Infantry Regiment.

RAF air reconnaissance spotted this large force on December 6, but the vessels were lost due to heavy cloud cover and generally deteriorating weather. At midday on December 7 a Catalina flying boat, searching for the elusive Japanese, became the first RAF casualty of the Pacific war. That day the Japanese transports split up, with 17 of them heading for a three-pronged landing in Malaya at Singora, Patani, and Kota Bharu. On the night of December 7/8, the first landings of the war began. British air attacks challenged the Japanese invasion by sinking one transport and damaging others, although the operation suffered no lasting disruption.

As Matsui's army poured into Malaya from the coastal landing points, British defenses crumbled. By December 15, a general withdrawal was ordered, effective immediately. Lt-Gen. Arthur R. Percival, GOC Malaya, had three divisions of IIIrd Indian Corps to oppose the Japanese advance into the Malay Peninsula, which was 175 miles wide in places. Masters of infiltration, Imperial troops easily circumvented British attempts to defend the roads by traversing swamps, rivers, and jungles—no natural barrier could seemingly hold them back.

Below: Taking the salute in pre-war Singapore's naval base perpetuated much of the traditional pomp and ceremony of British colonial rule.

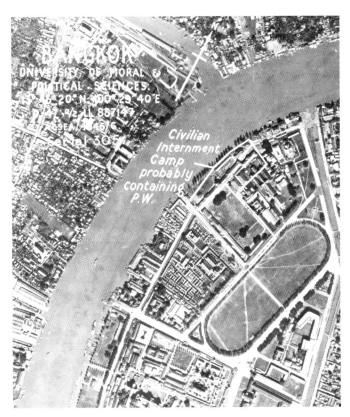

Fresh Indian and British troops who landed in Malaya did not necessarily alter the balance. Although they may have outnumbered the Japanese troops, without adequate training they could hardly be effective against seasoned jungle fighters. There were other reasons as well; men bound for other theaters suddenly finding themselves in the Far East were in no condition to fight after an exhausting sea voyage.

By December 17 a makeshift Malayan defense line had been drawn at the Perak River, although this was broken by the Imperial Army in a matter of days. The Japanese advance had reached Ipoh by December 26 and Kampar on January 2, 1942. On January 5, Japanese reinforcements were landed on the west coast of Malaya, and two days later a defense line at the Slim River had also been broken, this by a Japanese tank assault. A British defense of Kuala Lumpur was also unsuccessful, the town falling to the Japanese on January 17. Five days later, British forces at Muar had been smashed.

Western Desert veteran General Archibald Wavell, who was C-in-C ABDA (American, British, Dutch, Australian) Command, faced an impossible task. Hampered by poor communications, a tortuous chain of command, and newly arrived (but generally low grade) troop reinforcements, his responsibility encompassed virtually all Allied forces in Southeast Asia.

Below: The battlecruiser *Repulse*, sunk along with the *Prince of Wales* as the ill-fated "Force Z," made an impressive enough sight in home waters in 1935.

Unfamiliar with the area, Wavell could hardly keep pace with the speed at which the enemy was advancing and ruining any plans to hold various lines of defense. With British forces continuing to fall back southward toward Singapore, evacuations began.

There were isolated actions that gave momentary hope, only to be dashed as pockets of resistance were overwhelmed. An Australian stand at Gemma soon petered out before news of another retreat was received. This fed the general sense of hopelessness, a feeling already well advanced. Wavell noted with dismay the chaotic conditions in Singapore: reinforcements poured in, but with little idea of what they were supposed to do. At least 25,000 troops and their equipment had already been lost in Malaya, and although Percival had another 85,000 men under his command, many were ill-trained native volunteers.

At Singapore, General Yamashita (in overall command of the Malayan operation) finally laid to rest the myth of poor Oriental fighting ability. As three divisions of his Twenty-Fifth Army prepared to cross the causeway separating Singapore Island from the Malayan mainland, he ostensibly faced the strength of Percival's garrison, which outnumbered his own forces by more than two to one. However, no fortified positions could be observed and there was little riposte to Japanese artillery barrages.

Above: A very low level PR run over Rangoon jail on May 3, 1945, revealed PoWs—who often provided some visual confirmation of their presence after the Japanese had left in order to speed rescue.

Right: An Air Command Southeast Asia photo taken on January 3, 1945, showing the possible location of a PoW camp on the notorious River Kwai at Kanchanaburi.

Pre-war British estimations that an attack on Singapore would open with a seaborne assault had resulted in the island's main defense being vested primarily in naval guns which pointed out into the South China Sea. They were not needed—Japanese troops had come overland in tanks, on foot, riding bicycles and in captured trucks, to completely seal off the peninsula. By February 10, there were 30,000 Japanese troops on the island.

Percival withdrew to Singapore town where he had to contend with a million civilians. The enemy had, meanwhile, captured the town's unguarded water supply, and when Imperial Army tanks took Bukit Timah, further resistance seemed all but futile. Percival made surrender overtures to the Japanese and, on February 15, hostilities ceased. It had taken Yamashita just 70 days to conclude the Malayan operation, against the estimated 100. He had secured 130,000 prisoners, and had captured airfields, an almost undamaged naval base, and substantial natural assets including tin and rubber.

The loss of Singapore was, in Winston Churchill's words, "the most ignominious capitulation in the history of British arms." The victorious Japanese tended to agree. They regarded the spectacle of armed, able-bodied men surrendering en masse as beyond comprehension, an act totally devoid of all dignity. This Oriental view conveniently ignored the British desire to minimize casualties and save lives in what were considered hopeless acts of bravery, had resistance continued. The irony was that Allied casualties continued as the Japanese force-marched the prisoners to camps, denying them sufficient food and medical supplies. Percival himself was dispatched to Manchuria and survived to see the surrender of Japan.

The Malayan campaign was one of a series of Japanese victories representing one of the most outstanding feats of arms in the history of warfare. Britain's military defeat at Singapore fatally undermined her position as a colonial power, so

Right: The fate of 130,000 prisoners taken by the Japanese during the operations in Malaya—hard labor in Japanese prison camps; this one is in Thailand.

much so that it was never fully recovered. Indeed, this was the beginning of the end for a waning Empire.

In the opening days of the war, American forces hardly fared any better than their British counterparts. The same complacent attitude toward any threat from the East had largely prevailed in the Philippines and other American spheres of influence. Garrisons were poorly equipped, without modern arms, and in terms of manpower, too much reliance was placed on locally recruited troops, many of whom needed years of training to bring them to the required level of fighting efficiency.

ALLIED LOSSES AT SEA

At sea Japanese strength was as decisive as it was on land. Hugely boosted by the success of the Pearl Harbor operation, her navy dealt equally harshly with Allied attempts to challenge operations by Imperial forces. It became all too painfully clear to the Allies that the Japanese had—in a state of near-total secrecy—equipped their navy with excellent warships, their air forces with superbly capable aircraft, and instilled in their troops a spirit of nationalist fervor impossible for Western minds to comprehend. In short the Oriental, who had been dismissed as a lesser mortal, much inferior to the Caucasian, was now brutally mocking the folly of such attitudes.

Understandably alarmed at the apparent annihilation of the U.S. fleet at Pearl Harbor, the British Admiralty responded to the urging by Winston Churchill to dispatch capital ships to the Far East with all speed. The battlecruisers *Prince of Wales* and *Repulse* sailed as the core of "Force Z" and, on December 8, Admiral Sir Tom Phillips, C-in-C British Far Eastern Fleet, left Singapore with an escort of four destroyers. It was intended that the Royal Navy ships should attack Japanese landing points at Singora in Siam and Kota Bharu in Malaya. En route to

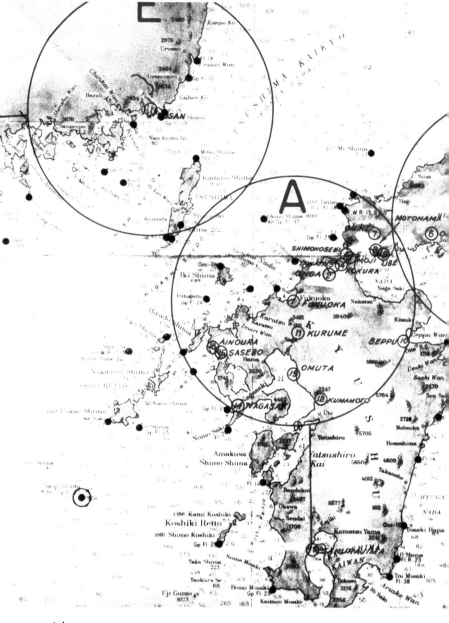

Above: A July 1945 map prepared by the U.S. Army's 64th Topographic Engineer Battalion showing the location of over 70 PoW camps in the Japanese home islands.

his operational area, on the 9th, Phillips was informed that no fighter cover was available in the Singora area and he reversed course, intending to return to Singapore; but the British warships had been spotted by Japanese aircraft.

In the evening of the 9th a signal received by the *Prince of Wales* indicated that enemy landings had taken place at Kuantan on the Malayan coast. Without informing Singapore of his decision, Phillips changed course and led Force Z towards this new danger point, his intention being, as before, to bombard enemy invasion transports. Keeping track of the warships, the Japanese Navy air command in Indo-China alerted crews of the 22nd Air Flotilla for an important mission.

in "line of sight" maneuvering and deployment of warships. This was particularly good at night, when fleet actions, sometimes backed up by searchlights, proved highly effective. As was demonstrated in a number of early war actions, Allied ships were disastrously out-gunned and out-maneuvered. U.S. ships also nursed an Achilles' heel in that they would often pour their useless, mainly steam-propelled torpedoes into the sea and hit the enemy at point-blank range, only to find that it was they who suffered the losses. Well-aimed and lethal Japanese torpedoes worked, whereas their own often failed to explode. No U.S. torpedo of anywhere near comparable quality to the Japanese "Long Lance" had even been tested by 1941.

For all their seeming efficiency in the early battles, the Japanese military lacked the excellent inter-service cooperation that was rapidly developed by the Allies; Imperial Army and Navy factions only occasionally operated together —rather, the two existed more as rivals, at times fighting what amounted to separate campaigns. Each service had its jealously guarded military budget and design departments which produced a whole series of weapons, particularly aircraft. This situation almost inevitably led to duplication of effort that dissipated industrial capacity.

As the force of G4M and G3M bombers droned southward on December 10, Admiral Phillips received confirmation that no landing had actually taken place at Kuantan. Then, at 11.00 hours, the first enemy aircraft were sighted.

By co-ordinating their torpedo and conventional bombing runs the Japanese swamped the British ships. Torpedoes hit first, *Prince of Wales* being badly damaged. The same fate awaited *Repulse*, which went down at 12.33. By 13.20 *Prince of Wales* had also capsized and sunk. The destroyers pulled over 2,000 survivors out of the South China Sea as a finale to Allied seapower dominance in the Far East for the time being. No battleships now remained in the Far East to challenge the Japanese Navy.

Although they were deficient in terms of some modern technology, particularly radar, the Japanese Navy had developed remarkable skills

As the war went on and the Allies gained the upper hand, such an atmosphere of rivalry did little to improve an increasingly bad military position, and the rift was not entirely healed even when the country was on the brink of utter defeat. By then operations to defend Iwo Jima and Okinawa forced a degree of cooperation on the Japanese, and the last kamikaze attacks finally saw the Japanese army and naval air forces operating together, but by then it was far too late.

JAPANESE HIGH POINT

2. THE LOSS OF THE PHILIPPINES AND BATTLE OF THE JAVA SEA

BACKGROUND

A U.S. possession since 1898, the Philippine Islands had always figured strongly in defense plans for the western Pacific. Pre-war projections of the difficulty of retaking the islands, should they be lost in the early stages of a future conflict, began uncannily to unfold almost exactly as predicted. When Japanese bombers appeared over Clark Field and other air bases on December 8, the ramshackle air defense of the islands was quickly whittled down to the point of impotency.

With the nearest Japanese naval base lying 1,500 miles away, and the forward base on Formosa even nearer at 600 miles distant, the vulnerability of the Philippines was clear enough. Should Japan attack in force, the sprawling group of 7,000 islands would be hard to defend without massive air and sea forces.

These the United States did not possess in 1941, although the fact was kept from the American public. Some attempt was, however, made to build up a defensive force when General Douglas MacArthur was appointed head of U.S. Army Forces in the Far East (USAFFE). Taking on responsibility for expanding the Philippine Army, MacArthur assured Washington that the islands could be defended. The opposite was true. Ill-prepared to face an invasion by a modern army, young Filipinos volunteered for military training while their government relied heavily on a U.S. presence, particularly that of army air units, for their national security.

Optimistically dismissing the possibility of any Japanese attack in the Pacific until at least

Below: Japanese airfield at Cape Gloucester on New Britain photographed on September 4, 1943.

Above: U.S. Navy aircraft dispersed on Munda airfield in the Solomons.

the spring of 1942, MacArthur awaited the delivery of substantial quantities of arms. A shortage of transports hampered this, but to his credit the number of troops did increase significantly. By December 8, 1941, there were 31,000 men available, including the Filipino Scout formation which served in the U.S. Army. Indigenous divisions raised the total to 110,000 men, although these were generally still under training and only basically equipped.

Modern air power in the Philippines was almost entirely in American hands, the indigenous PAF flying obsolete aircraft. The USAAF had earlier based early-model Boeing B-17D and Douglas B-18 bombers, plus Seversky P-35 and Curtiss P-40 fighters, at Clark, Nichols, and Iba fields—these forces became one of the prime Japanese targets.

As the IJN's A6Ms would be needed to escort the long-range bombers which formed the Philippines air strike force, tests were conducted to determine the leanest possible engine fuel settings. By adopting this technique the "Zeke" pilots had been able to stretch their range to about 1,000 miles. Even so, occupying

Bataan, a small island 150 miles north of Luzon, on the first day of the assault was a wise precaution as the fighters were able to refuel there on their return from operations over Luzon and the Philippines.

It was with some trepidation that the Japanese aircrews approached Luzon at midday on December 8, as it was assumed that the earlier attack on Pearl Harbor would have put the defenders on full alert. The IJN aircrews had been delayed by fog over the Formosa airfields, and they fully expected to be bombed themselves. The news from Pearl Harbor brought only confusion and indecision at the U.S. headquarters on Luzon—where should the B-17s attack? A bombing mission to Formosa was changed to a PR flight; when this returned the bombing would finally go ahead. It was past midday and refueling was still underway as the first Japanese aircraft arrived over Clark Field. The Zero pilots went about their deadly

Above: A USAAF B-25 Mitchell laying smoke to cover a breach in an enemy steel girder beach obstacle made by U.S./Australian troops in Borneo on April 30, 1943.

Below: Under cover of the smokescreen, engineers attach charges to the beach obstacles.

work as the Navy bomb aimers set their sights. They were hardly challenged, and in a matter of hours the Far East Air Force almost ceased to exist.

INVASION

While the JNAF and JAAF pounded the remaining air bases in the islands, and attacked any shipping found in Manila Bay and at the Cavite naval base, multiple invasion forces had set out for the Philippines on December 9. The northernmost thrust, commanded by Rear-Adm. Raizo Tanaka, headed for landing points above Lingayen Gulf to put 2,000 troops ashore at Apari, Vigan, Buang, and Iba. Lt-Gen. Homma Masaharu's main Fourteenth Army contingent of 7,000 men had sailed from the Ryukyu Islands on December 9–10, and on the 22nd had landed on southern Luzon. Driving rapidly inland, they were quickly able to threaten the capital Manila.

On December 12, 2,500 troops under Maj-Gen. Naoki Kimura landed at Legaspi from their Palau embarkation points, and on the 19th a second force from Palau set foot on the largest southern Philippine island of Mindanao, transports forming a secondary prong of this force simultaneously breaking away towards the Sulu Archipelago to attack Borneo.

These multiple landings, designed to wreck Allied communications throughout the Philippines, capture air bases, and generally disrupt the cohesion of any defense, went very much according to plan. Largely denied air cover, the Philippine Army's two divisions and the scouts of the 26th Cavalry opposed the Japanese as best they could. Hampered by lack of military equipment, particularly artillery, the Filipinos began to retreat towards Baguio, the summer capital.

To prevent the Japanese making heavy air raids on the capital, MacArthur declared Manila an open city on December 24. He evacuated to Corregidor, lying at the mouth of Manila Bay, there to make a final stand—but troops of the rapidly advancing Japanese Fourteenth Army ruined that plan. A further withdrawal to Bataan then took place, a move that gained a breathing space for the defenders, who eventually numbered some 90,000 men. Manila fell to the Japanese on January 2, 1942.

MacArthur's defense line, running from Mauben in the west to Mabating on Manila Bay, was attacked by the green 65th Brigade, with which Homma had been saddled as a replacement unit when his experienced 48th Division had been transferred away. Believing the American defense line to be weak, the Japanese general felt he could risk deploying the newcomers, in spite of their inexperience.

They found the defenders much tougher than anticipated. Two corps, commanded by Maj-Gen. Jonathan Wainwright to the west and by Maj-Gen. George Parker in the east, constituted the main line of defense. Respective strengths of these corps were: the 1st, 31st, and 91st Philippine Army (PA) Divisions plus the 26th Cavalry under Wainwright, and the 11th, 21st, 41st, and 51st PA Divisions and the 57th Philippine Scout Regiment under Parker.

The American and Filipino forces had other problems, however. There were few medical supplies to cope with a rising rate of sickness from malaria, beriberi, and dysentery, food stocks were running low, and Washington appeared all but deaf to the pleas from MacArthur for reinforcements, something that did nothing to boost morale. Submarines were the only vessels able to slip through the IJN blockade and they managed to deliver some essentials, but nowhere near what was needed.

However, when the Japanese attacked on January 9, the defenders felt confident enough. The front line was bisected by the 4,000-foot Mount Natib, and it was believed that the mountain would be all but impassable. For six days the defenses held while the enemy worked around Natib. Then a breakthrough in the 51st Division sector threatened to outflank Parker.

Wainwright's force also came under threat, and on January 24 MacArthur ordered a withdrawal eight miles south, by which time both sides were almost exhausted. The Japanese 65th Brigade had lost a quarter of its strength, and despite MacArthur's vow to "fight it out to complete destruction," the situation was clearly hopeless.

When Homma made three amphibious landings behind the American lines, and especially when the Japanese commander combined this new threat with a frontal assault by his 16th Division, Wainwright's positions were overrun. Homma, however, his remaining troops racked by sickness, was forced to cease operations

Above: Milne Bay in New Guinea became an important Allied base. Held by Australians, it also provided a useful harbor for U.S. PT boats.

Left: Typical conditions in New Guinea see Australian and U.S. troops being helped by Papuan natives.

pending the arrival of reinforcements. He laid siege to Bataan for nearly two months, and not before April 3 was it lifted to end in another Allied defeat. MacArthur was ordered to leave for Australia; he did so on March 11, pledging to return. Wainwright assumed command in the Philippines.

In late March Homma got his reinforcements; the 14th and part of the 21st Division were now supported by artillery and air units. The final attack came early in April. The fatally weakened defense collapsed and Maj-Gen. Edward King, commanding officer on Luzon, decided to surrender—despite an order from MacArthur to counter-attack. Estimating such a move to be tantamount to suicide for his emaciated forces, King surrendered on April 9. The cruel irony was that these men were then forced to walk

into captivity—the notorious Bataan Death March had begun.

By early May General Homma still had not taken Manila harbor, which was dominated by the 10,000-strong garrison on Corregidor. The Japanese subjected the fortress to a sustained land, air, and sea bombardment lasting almost a month, by which time the defenders, many of whom had taken refuge in the Malinta Tunnel, were desperate for food, water, medical supplies, and ammunition. Rallying for a final effort, the defenders awaited the inevitable Japanese attack. When this came on the night of May 5/6, Homma's troops sustained heavy casualties.

Remorselessly pushing forward, the Japanese fought through the night, and when tanks appeared in the morning of the 6th, the defenders knew they were finally beaten. They had no anti-tank weapons and there were about 1,000 wounded in the Malinta Tunnel. It was largely to save them being massacred that Wainwright opted to surrender.

Further Japanese landings made the capture of the entire Philippines only a matter of time—but with isolated units holding out, they insisted that Wainwright's capitulation should mean that all fighting troops should capitulate. Having

Above: One of many landing points utilized by the Allies along the New Guinea coast, Oro Bay shows a typical landing stage for supply freighters.

themselves taken some 12,000 casualties and inflicted about 16,000 on the American and Filipino defenders, the campaign had been the most costly the Japanese had yet undertaken. The surrender of Corregidor netted them another 84,000 prisoners of war. Thousands were to die at the harsh hands of their captors.

Perceived pre-war as a major disaster for the United States, the loss of the Philippines turned out to be strategically less important for the future prosecution of the war than had been anticipated. The fighting had also shown that the Japanese Army, far from being "invincible," could be held by a determined and well-equipped force. Notwithstanding the final victory, the Japanese high command had little choice but to swallow this bitter pill and General Homma, who had taken three months longer than planned to secure victory in the Philippines, was relieved.

BATTLE OF THE JAVA SEA

At the conclusion of their operations against Singapore on February 15, the Japanese prepared to secure the chain of islands constituting the Malay barrier, the Dutch East Indies. Of these Borneo, Sumatra, and Java were the most important to the Allies. Defended by mixed Allied forces, some hardly strong enough to resist the invaders, all had fallen to the Japanese by March.

The Dutch Rear-Adm. Karel Doorman vowed to wreck enemy plans to take Java and prepared a three-wave attack on the Japanese troop transports. Poor coordination spoiled a potentially successful first strike, with the enemy rapidly offsetting a numerical inferiority by sinking a Dutch destroyer and damaging the cruiser *Tromp*.

For two days Doorman impatiently waited for positive confirmation of the whereabouts of the enemy—then, just as his fleet was heading back to Surabaya for rest and replenishment, a report confirmed his quarry west of Bawean Island. Doorman set off to rendezvous with the enemy ships, the ensuing clash becoming known as the Battle of the Java Sea. For the Dutch admiral and many Allied sailors, the engagement represented yet another disaster.

A mixed cruiser squadron, comprising the Dutch *De Ruyter* and *Java*, the British *Exeter*, the USS *Houston*, and the Australian *Perth*, covered by nine destroyers, prepared to do battle. In column formation the Allied vessels opened fire at 28,000 yards on the IJN ships, which were in two groups of four cruisers with a strong destroyer escort. Return fire from the Japanese scored few hits until an eight-inch shell struck *Exeter* and forced her to retire.

By abruptly turning out of formation, the British cruiser created confusion: thinking that Doorman had ordered the entire column to turn, the Allied cruisers presented their broadsides to the enemy. It was indeed lucky that only one Dutch destroyer was lost to the enemy's answering fire.

When darkness fell the Allied ships suffered further loss when a British destroyer sank in a minefield. Steaming north, Doorman encountered the IJN ships again. Fire was exchanged followed by salvoes of Long Lance torpedoes. Some of these found *De Ruyter* and *Java*, both of which sank.

The surviving Allied ships limped back to Batavia, and the decision was then taken to withdraw all Allied vessels from the Java Sea—if they could evade the strong Japanese forces covering all the exits. Four U.S. destroyers did break

Below: The U.S. Fifth Air Force pioneered the technique of skip bombing enemy ships from masthead height. This Japanese destroyer has been stricken by B-25s dropping 500lb bombs to ricochet lethally across the water.

out to reach Australia, but *Exeter* was discovered making for Sundra Strait and was sunk along with two escorting destroyers. A similar fate awaited *Houston* and *Perth* which went down after a fierce battle with Japanese cruisers.

ATTACK ON AUSTRALIA

As well as winning numerous localized victories over opposing navies, the Japanese maintained pressure on land targets. They realized that Australia, at the eastern end of the Malay barrier, represented a potentially great danger to future operations as and when Allied air and sea reinforcements arrived. In an attempt to pin down forces that might otherwise be used against them, the Imperial planners ordered a heavy air raid on Darwin on February 19. Bombers of the 21st Air Flotilla based in the Celebes were escorted by Nagumo's carrier fighters which were launched in the Timor Sea. These aircraft pounded the port and adjacent airfield, and Darwin town was also heavily damaged, resulting in 5,000 casualties. Eleven ships were destroyed in the harbor and 23 aircraft wrecked on the ground.

Although the raid on Darwin was followed by others, the Japanese knew that Australia was beyond their grasp; the ten divisions they would have needed to mount an effective invasion simply were not available. For the Japanese there was little alternative to this other than to continue raids, hope to contain Allied retaliation from Australia, and seek a decisive victory over the most dangerous enemy surface ships, principally the American carriers. To this end an elaborate plan to draw the U.S. Navy into such a decisive action moved into high gear. The key question was about which location the Americans would consider important enough to defend by committing the bulk of their fleet. Samoa, Fiji, and New Caledonia were considered, but the choice finally fell on the tiny, strategically important island of Midway. Under IJN planning, the U.S. garrison on the island would be destroyed and an invasion force would

Right: Marching through the typical vegetation of New Guinea's Ramu Valley, an Australian patrol shows the individual option of wearing either a steel helmet or bush hat.

Below: LSTs—Landing Ships, Transport—could bring in vehicles, men, and supplies of all kinds. Such deliveries of war materiel were a decisive factor in Allied victory.

simultaneously land in the Aleutians—and the American fleet, lured into combat to defend Midway, would be destroyed.

RAIDS INTO THE INDIAN OCEAN

In the meantime, Kondo and Ozawa directed carrier raids into the Indian Ocean. Designed to keep the Allies off balance and to destroy warships that could not quickly be replaced, these air and surface attacks appeared to indicate a dangerous new phase of the war. IJN submarines also sank a significant tonnage of Allied shipping during this period.

Meanwhile, Admiral of the Fleet Sir Dudley Pound had brought together elements of a new Eastern Fleet. Under the command of Admiral Sir James Somerville, the fleet sortied from Ceylon on April 4 to avoid being bombed while in port, having been forewarned that the Japanese planned such a raid. On April 5, bombs indeed rained down on Colombo. Some of the British ships were found by enemy carrier aircraft later that day, and *Dorsetshire* and

Cornwall, the fleet's only cruisers, were both sunk.

Four days later a more serious British loss in the Indian Ocean was that of the carrier *Hermes*, which was then underway from Trincomalee covered by a small task group. The escort ships failed to withstand attack by the highly experienced aircrew from three IJN carriers, who also sent a destroyer, a corvette, and two tankers to the bottom. The loss of *Hermes*, despite her modest size and probably limited tactical value, nevertheless meant a temporary curtailment to RN carrier operations in the Indian Ocean area.

Unknown to the Japanese, the two most capable British fleet carriers, *Indomitable* and *Formidable*, were at the time of the attack on Ceylon, safely berthed at their "secret" base at Addu Atoll in the Maldives. These carriers would return to the fray in due course. This was not the case for the Japanese; on April 12 the Combined Fleet returned to Kure and, although Admirals Kondo and Ozawa would see further active service in the Pacific, there were no further incursions into the Indian Ocean in strength.

CONTAINMENT

As the momentum of the Japanese offensive perceptibly slowed, the Allies were finally able to enjoy a breathing space. There was an urgent need to develop new command structures to direct future strategy and operations across the entire spectrum of the Pacific Ocean Area and Southeast Asia. Compromised to some degree by the priority calls on units, equipment, and, indeed, experienced commanders and field officers from Europe, the Pacific theater nevertheless had to be urgently reorganized from the shambles that the Japanese had created. During much of 1943 the Japanese also tended to consolidate their gains, enabling the Allies to also make good the losses of the early war campaigns.

With the obvious prerequisite of earmarking those Japanese-held islands that needed to be retaken to provide bases and secure their own rear areas, the U.S. command also identified enemy-held territory that could be bypassed. It became advantageous not to dilute the main thrusts by needless diversions which would have been time-consuming and wasteful in lives and equipment. With increasing sea and air superiority over the Pacific, the U.S. could afford to conduct an aerial blockade of Rabaul on New Britain and other locations where small garrisons could be prevented from becoming a threat and gradually reduced in strength without the need for an invasion.

Right: Gaping bow doors of well camouflaged LSTs disgorging trucks and supplies on the north shore of Huon Gulf east of Lae in New Guinea.

THE ROAD BACK

3. CORAL SEA, MIDWAY, SOLOMONS, AND MARIANAS

BACKGROUND

As a curtain raiser to the subsequent clash at Midway, a U.S. task force (built around the carriers *Yorktown* and *Lexington*) sortied in April 1942 to prevent the Japanese invading Port Moresby in New Guinea. To counter any Allied reaction and protect its invasion transports, the IJN sailed from Truk with a strong force including the carriers *Zuikaku*, *Shokaku*, and *Shoho*. Quick reaction by American and Australian airmen put enough transports on the bottom of the Coral Sea to thwart the invasion; the battle thus saved a vitally important forward base from which air operations in the Southwest Pacific—these often originating in Australia—were being conducted, albeit on a modest scale.

BATTLE OF THE CORAL SEA

Under the command of Rear-Adm. Frank Jack Fletcher, Task Force 17 conducted a search for the Japanese on May 2. Flying his flag in *Yorktown*, Fletcher received news of Japanese landings at Tulagi in the Solomons and headed north, but on May 4 he reversed course to rendezvous with Admiral Fitch (aboard *Lexington*) and refuel his ships. Meanwhile, the Japanese carrier striking force under Vice-Adm. Takagi and Admiral Hara had entered the Coral Sea.

On May 7, Fletcher sent his Cruiser Support Group to attack the enemy landing force heading for Port Moresby. Japanese air reconnaissance then sighted the U.S. cruisers, but shortly after 08.00 the Americans picked up Takagi's carriers. Fletcher began launching air strikes at 09.26 and these continued for over an hour. The SBDs and TBDs sighted *Shoho* and attacked immediately with bombs and torpedoes. Zigzagging violently in a vain attempt to escape the

Right: A target photograph of Wake Island taken by aircraft of U.S. Navy light escort carrier USS *Cowpens* (CVL-25) during an attack on June 20, 1945.

Above: White phosphorous bombs make their characteristic mushroom cloud of white smoke during the second U.S. Navy strike on Wake Island.

onslaught, the enemy carrier slipped beneath the waves at 11.35. Japanese pilots failed to find any American targets after a 16.30 launch from *Shokaku* and *Zuikaku* ordered by Admiral Hara.

On May 8, the Americans found *Shokaku* and *Zuikaku*—just as the IJN airmen sighted *Lexington* and *Saratoga*. Almost simultaneously both sides launched air strikes and attacked their respective targets between 10.57 and 11.18. The result was that *Shokaku* was very badly damaged and all but put out of action, although she remained afloat. *Lexington*, previously damaged by a torpedo, suffered a series of crippling explosions just after midday. The carrier was clearly doomed, and was abandoned at 17.10 to be finally sunk by a U.S. torpedo. The Americans then withdrew, while Admiral Takagi dispatched *Shokaku* back to Truk for repairs

Seemingly a draw, as both sides lost a carrier, the Coral Sea engagement was more an American than a Japanese victory, because the latter failed in its purpose for the first time. Being prevented from landing troops at Moresby was one of the factors that finally proved fatal to Japan's war aims. The enormous task of securing Port Moresby's airfields and adjacent harbor was thus handed to the army, which faced the prospect of an arduous overland campaign along the Kokoda Trail.

BATTLE OF MIDWAY

Convinced that he could trap the American fleet into a decisive showdown, Admiral Yamamoto sortied for Midway Island in June 1942. Bent on winning as decisive a victory at sea as Imperial troops had achieved on land, the admiral had a mighty fleet at his back. Banking much on the element of surprise, Yamamoto was unaware that his movements were known to the Americans, who had recently broken the IJN's communications code—the intercepts of which were codenamed "Magic."

Being able to read the enemy's coded messages was a major breakthrough for the U.S. Having a good idea where the Japanese ships were and what their commanders' immediate plans were offered the possibility of inflicting a decisive defeat which would, at least, stem the rampage of the Japanese Navy throughout the Pacific. As the Battle of the Coral Sea had shown, U.S. airmen were more than capable of sinking the IJN carriers if they could get to grips with them.

With Midway more than a slim possibility of becoming the IJN's next major target, Pacific Fleet commander Chester W. Nimitz, who had assumed that office on December 31, 1941, had flown out there on May 2 to see for himself the state of the island's defenses. On receiving "Magic" confirmation that the IJN was indeed intending to take Midway, he ordered Raymond Spruance to take over Task Force 16 from "Bill" Halsey, who was ill. The carriers constituting TF-16—*Enterprise* and *Hornet*—left Pearl Harbor on May 28, Fletcher's TF-17 with *Yorktown* slipping anchor on the 30th. Admiral Nagumo's force had sailed on the 27th, while Yamamoto put to sea on the 28th.

Above: Bombs dropped by USS *Hancock*'s air group explode on Wake Island in the fourth raid the Navy made on the island.

Naval intelligence in 1942 was not such a precise science that local air reconnaissance could be dispensed with completely, and on May 3 a patrolling Catalina from Midway detected the IJN carriers. The message, "Many planes headed Midway," confirmed without any doubt that the tiny atoll was the enemy target, and was passed on to the carriers. The pivotal battle of the Pacific war was starting.

Having put great store on being able to take up their battle positions in secrecy, the IJN admirals were alarmed to see the PBYs. If Nagumo needed any further confirmation that the Americans now knew his carriers were off Midway, the afternoon of the 3rd dispelled it. Bombs from B-17s based on the atoll were aimed at his fleet, although all of them missed. Nagumo acted and launched an initial strike on Midway, lying some 280 miles northwest of his ships.

The Midway engagement appeared not to start well for the U.S. forces, as bombers of Nagumo's Mobile Fleet plastered the island's runway, dispersals, and installations. Most U.S. aircraft had taken off beforehand, however, and few machines were destroyed on the ground. The worst loss was among the defending fighters which clashed with the incoming strike's "Zeke" escort, 17 U.S. aircraft going down for six Japanese.

The Japanese carrier force returned to replenish with fuel and switch to torpedoes and HE bombs for a second strike, anticipating the appearance of the American carriers, although the commanders had no definite location report at that time. A serious defect in Japanese planning for the Midway operation was a poorly planned air search and consequent failure to detect Spruance's carriers early enough.

As the dust cleared on Midway, the island garrison launched six of the new Grumman TBF Avenger torpedo bombers to attack the Mobile Fleet. All but one fell before the guns and fighter cover of the carriers. Another try by the AAF, which desperately launched Martin Marauders rigged as torpedo bombers, also failed to score any hits. Neither did Midway-based B-17s manage to hit any of the enemy ships in a second conventional high-level bombing mission. These disappointing AAF sorties passed the torch almost entirely to naval units.

By adopting sound tactics which dovetailed intelligence data, reconnaissance, and strike resources, the U.S. Navy carrier commanders planned well in order to offset any advantage the enemy might possess. For their part, the Japanese went into battle with less factual information than the Americans. They were bolstered by total confidence in the outcome of any battle,

Above: A billowing screen of phosphorous smoke obscures much of Wake during the fourth U.S. Navy strike.

but dangerously false optimism was no recipe for success.

With reports of an American carrier sighting in his hands by 08.20, Nagumo took a difficult decision: with his Midway strike force returning he would wait to bring them aboard before heading north. With the prospect of a carrier strike in the offing, he ordered his air groups to replace the previously hung HE bombs with armour-piercing types. The bombs removed from the waiting aircraft were stacked on deck to save time. As he turned onto a new course, the Japanese admiral saw an air raid coming in.

Considerable U.S. optimism had accompanied the launching of the Devastator torpedo bombers from *Hornet*. Dangerously slow and vulnerable to fighter attack though they were, the TBDs were the only aircraft in the carrier air groups capable of torpedo attack. Joined by aircraft from *Enterprise* and *Yorktown*, the TBDs were singularly unsuccessful. Going in on the enemy ships, all but one of the Devastators of Torpedo Squadron Eight (VT-8) were wiped out by the "Zeke" CAP and naval gunfire. Rear-seat Observer Ensign T. Gray escaped from his ditched aircraft, took to his dinghy, and watched the entire Battle of Midway unfold in the skies above him.

By 10.15 Nagumo's pilots had fended off a potentially crippling series of U.S. torpedo attacks and had shot down 83 enemy aircraft. In the meantime the Dauntlesses of TF-16 had also launched, to begin what became a lengthy search for the Japanese fleet. By 08.30 TF-17 had also launched 35 dive bombers from *Yorktown* to boost the strike force to 151 aircraft.

Receipt of an erroneous position report confused things, and it was almost two hours before the SBD crews finally spotted their quarry. The Japanese gun crews, then concentrating their fire on another wave of low-flying Devastators, failed to notice the high-level threat. The Dauntlesses pushed over into their steep dives from 20,000 feet to release their 500lb bombs. These caused enormous damage among the aircraft of the Japanese air groups, fueled and bombed-up on the decks of the carriers. Chain-reaction explosions tore the heart out of the *Akagi*, *Shokaku*, and *Soryu*. Parked above and below decks, the IJN aircraft turned into blazing torches, helping to seal the fate of their own ships.

The *Akagi* went first, Nagumo and his staff leaving the stricken carrier at 10.46. *Kaga*, meanwhile, became a blazing inferno, while *Soryu* also burned, her rudder and engines out of action. *Hiryu*, still able to operate aircraft, sent off a strike which found *Yorktown* and, despite having 12 aircraft in the attack shot down, two bombs struck home. Losing all way at 12.20, *Yorktown* got underway again, but a second wave of *Hiryu* aircraft put two torpedoes into her and the carrier had to be abandoned.

Spruance then sent 24 Dauntlesses after the remaining Japanese carrier, and these found her shortly before 17.00. Pounding along at 33 knots, *Hiryu* still could not avoid hits by four bombs, which caused devastation on the flight-deck. About two hours later *Hiryu* went down, as did *Kaga*.

Midway was the classic carrier engagement, arguably never equaled in history. In the space of a few minutes it robbed the Japanese fleet of the core of its deadly seaborne striking force and hundreds of its finest naval aviators.

Blessed with the idefinable element of luck, the American attack was pressed home with courage against an equal enemy, suddenly fighting for his life. There were, apart from the "traditional" sacrifices of Captain Aoki of *Akagi* and Yamaguchi of *Hiryu* who insisted of going down with their ships, few wasteful heroics on the part of the Japanese, no senseless sacrifice of well-trained men. Midway was an undeniable vindication of carrier airpower in which no sailor on either side sighted the opposing ships. It was a simple matter of luck—had the U.S. dive bombers not found them first, the Japanese might well have inflicted a similar scale of loss on the American carriers. As it was, the IJN never made good the loss of its four most capable carriers while the Americans marked Midway as the first decisive victory of the Pacific war.

ALEUTIANS

Part of the Japanese plan for the overall Midway operation was to occupy the Aleutian Islands, and on June 7, 1942, the IJN sortied into the North Pacific to land troops on Kiska. In more than a year of occupation they would achieve little strategic gain on this inhospitable chain of islands. On May 11, 1943, the U.S. 7th Infantry Division landed on Attu and secured the island by the end of June. Partly based in the islands, the Eleventh Air Force carried out a difficult war of attrition but was instrumental in helping ground troops to mop up the enemy garrison.

Deciding to evacuate rather than fight, the Japanese pulled 5,000 troops off Kiska under a not unusual blanket of Aleutian fog. There had never been enough troops available to them to hold onto the Aleutians, which were regarded as a secondary theater by both sides. The Americans, however, utilized air bases in the region to assist in sending war material, particularly aircraft, to the Russians.

SOLOMONS

Far more dangerous to the Japanese were the U.S. Marine landings on Guadalcanal in the Solomon Islands two months after Midway. The Japanese had themselves established a foothold in the Solomons on May 2 when Operation "Mo" put troops ashore on the small island of Tulagi. A few days later, construction troops moved onto Guadalcanal and began to build an airfield.

Left: Close inspection of Wake Island target photos (taken from an altitude of 10,000ft here) revealed details of the Japanese-held airfield with numerous taxiways and circular revetments for dispersed aircraft.

Above Right: The Navy air strike of June 20, 1945, caused widespread damage on Wake Island.

The disaster at Midway forced a change of emphasis for the "Mo" plan, which now focused mainly on supporting the overland campaign to take Port Moresby. The Americans, realizing that an operational enemy airfield on Guadalcanal could cause them serious problems in the Southwest Pacific, opted to invade and capture it.

A hurriedly assembled U.S. Navy force was put together for Operation "Watchtower." It comprised Admiral Kelly Turner's amphibious task force and Fletcher's carrier and escort group; Maj-Gen. Alexander A. Vendregrift's 1st Marine Division, plus the 2nd Battalion, 5th Marines, 1st Raider and 1st Parachute Battalions, represented a force of about 19,000 men.

Storming ashore on August 7 in a move that took the Japanese by surprise, the Marines experienced little opposition on the beaches of either of the islands. In spite of the garrison on Tulagi holding out for three days, the first phase of "Watchtower" succeeded without heavy American casualties.

The fact that the Japanese construction gangs on Guadalcanal fled and left their heavy equipment behind greatly helped the Americans to complete the airfield. Much of their own construction equipment had not been unloaded from Admiral Turner's ships when a hurried departure was made from the island on August 9. Japanese retaliation dangerously exposed the fleet to air and surface attack, and at that critical point of the war, there was an overriding necessity to avoid losses.

Left to their own devices, the Marines prepared to make do with the supplies they had; enemy air attacks disrupted resupply to the point where much materiel was simply dumped on the beaches. Neither had all the troops managed to get ashore before the Navy pulled out—and there was little chance of reinforcements for the foreseeable future.

As Maj-Gen. Millard F. Harmon, commanding U.S. Army forces in the South Pacific, told Washington that the campaign to secure the Solomons was equal in importance to Midway for the future prosecution of the war. The victor would have a strategically important series of air bases and seaports for the duration of combat operations in the Southwest Pacific.

On August 18, the day that Guadalcanal's airfield was completed (it was named Henderson Field after a pilot killed at Midway), the Japanese made their move to win it back. Part of the 28th Infantry Regiment was landed by warship. Two days later, the first U.S. Marine fighters and dive bombers landed.

Airpower was the key to holding the islands, and the tough fight by the handful of U.S. Army and Marine fighters and bombers, collectively known as the "Cactus Air Force," to retain tenancy of Henderson Field, succeeded in thwarting all Japanese attempts to dislodge it. The pilots and groundcrew occupying the most important of the air bases in the Solomons were bombed, shelled, and subjected to suicidal troop assaults for many dangerous months.

For their part, the Japanese were committed to running a constant stream of supplies and reinforcement troops down to the Solomons from Rabaul and Truk. Known to the Americans as the "Tokyo Express," this service often succeeded in not only delivering the goods to the island defenders, but was capable of meting out short, sharp bombardments that killed Allied personnel, wrecked precious aircraft, and destroyed supplies. The warships that ran the "Express" were often led by their C-in-C, Rear-Adm. Raizo Tanaka. Nicknamed "Tenacious" for his untiring efforts to deliver supplies to the Solomons garrisons, Tanaka was later relieved of his command for protesting about the wasteful losses of ships.

A series of naval engagements off the Solomons, including the Battles of the Eastern Solomons, Cape Esperence, Santa Cruz, and Tassafaronga, brought losses to both sides, but eventually the IJN realized that it would be bled dry if it continued to run the gauntlet of the enemy's surface ships and aircraft. Although the land fighting was savage, the Americans were faced with relatively small numbers of Japanese at any one time. The "Tokyo Express" could only cram a finite number of troops aboard warships, and when these landed, the defenders were able to deal with them. Colonel Kiyono Ichiki, commander of the island forces, grew increasingly frustrated at the constant failure to dislodge the Americans and committed suicide. Japanese troops were continually wasted in these small scale battles.

Having lost the initiative and the means to mount a full-scale invasion, the Japanese high command eventually deemed there to be little future gain in further attempts to hold onto the Solomons. In January 1943 the Imperial Navy began quietly evacuating the surviving troops.

Japan, having reached far into the Southwest Pacific islands, now found increasing difficulty in maintaining these far-flung bases in the face of American and Allied counter-blows. The only option was to consolidate and pull out of territories which could not realistically be held. That process began in the Solomons, and by mid-1943, with further withdrawals having had to be made, the war situation in the Pacific slowly but surely turned against Japan.

Before 1943 was half over, the Japanese, having progressively abandoned Buna, Gona, and Guadalcanal to the Allies, with Kiska and Attu following in June, gradually went onto the defensive. The cost of operations—many of which were to resupply the still high number of garrisons established in the shrinking outer defense perimeter—was still rising alarmingly.

On March 2, 1943, an attempt had been made to put a sizeable force ashore to reinforce the important IJN airfield at Lae in New Guinea. Allied reaction was fast and deadly. Subject to a series of air attacks by the Fifth AAF and the RAAF that sent ship after ship to the bottom of the Bismarck Sea, Allied airmen were handed a secondary, much grimmer task. Knowing full well that every Japanese soldier who managed to swim ashore represented a threat to sorely stretched Allied troops, the aircraft skippers were told to strafe the men in the water.

Determined to strike back decisively, Yamamoto took command of Operation "I-Go," which was designed to neutralize Allied air bases and shipping in the Solomons and New Guinea areas. He deployed around 170 bombers and 200

Below: White phosphorous smoke blankets enemy AAA batteries on Wake's Peacock Point.

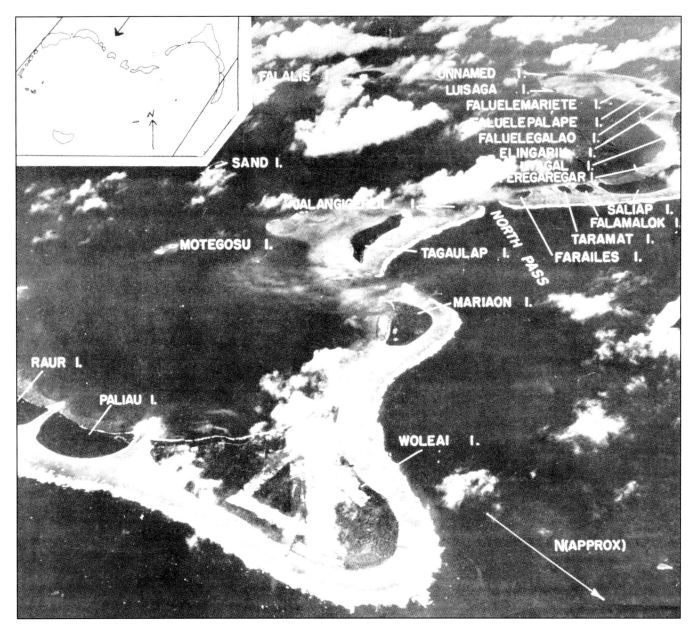

Above: Annotated target approach photo of the Woleai Islands on February 25, 1944, with the salient atolls being used by the Japanese clearly marked.

fighters, his first target being Guadalcanal on April 7. A large air battle above Savo Island saw the U.S. Marine fighters knock down 21 of the enemy, although the Allies suffered the loss of the destroyer *Aaron Ward*, a New Zealand Navy corvette, and an oiler. On the 11th the IJN dive bombers attacked shipping in Oro Bay and sank three vessels. Port Moresby's airfields were raided the following day with more follow up strikes on shipping. Believing the glowing but highly optimistic reports of Allied losses filed by his aircrews, Yamamoto prematurely called off "I-Go." He was due to undertake an inspection tour new air bases on Bougainville in two days' time.

DEATH OF YAMAMOTO

Allied intelligence was well aware that Japanese Navy successes owed much to the sound tactics evolved by Isoroku Yamamoto, and when "Magic" intercepts gave details of the itinerary of his tour, it seemed an ideal chance to remove the "architect of Pearl Harbor" from the scene. Yamamoto was warned that the naval codes might be compromised, but he set out nevertheless. On April 18, 18 P-38 Lightnings of the Thirteenth Air Force flew 550 miles from Guadalcanal to rendezvous with two "Betty" bombers carrying the admiral and his staff. Carving through the six "Zeke" fighters escorting the bombers, the P-38s shot down both the "Bettys." Yamamoto was killed by gunfire and the aircraft in which he was a passenger plunged into the jungle. His remains were later retrieved and Yamamoto awarded a state funeral (only the second commoner in Japanese history to have one). The loss of their greatest naval commander was a terrible blow and one from which the Japanese were never fully to recover.

Yamamoto's command was taken over by Admiral Minichi Koga, but he could hardly be expected to replicate the drive or the esteem enjoyed by his predecessor. The effect on the morale of the Japanese Navy was significant, for there was no true replacement for Yamamoto.

Throughout mid-1943 further naval engagements off the Solomons brought new disasters to the IJN. Overland operations in New Guinea became increasingly slow and difficult for the Japanese Army, which met tough resistance. Australian troops fought a gruelling campaign in some of the harshest jungle in the world, forcing the Japanese to give ground despite a series of counter-attacks on Australian Army positions at Kokoda.

While their land operations were disrupted by Allied troops, the Japanese were subjected to constant air attack. Their own forces tried valiantly, but with limited success, to counter a spiraling sortie rate by U.S. medium and light bombers, which were particularly deadly to ground troops and installations. The Fifth Air Force's energetic commander, George Kenney, having introduced modifications to turn his B-25 Mitchells and A-20 Havocs into heavily armed, low-flying strafers, had added new offensive techniques: skip bombing dealt with ships, and fragmentation bombs, dropped by parachute to delay the explosion while the aircraft got clear, devastated land targets. "Parafrags" destroyed parked aircraft, AAA gun positions, and numerous buildings.

American fighters—such as the P-38 Lightning, P-47 Thunderbolt, and the later-model P-40 Warhawks—fought air battles which on occasions were very one-sided, with poorly protected Japanese aircraft falling like flies. The Lightning became a particularly deadly foe, able as it was to out-range and out-gun

Above Right: A map of the Woleai Islands picking out items of interest adjacent to the main airfield, including an RDF station, a weather and radio station on Mariaon, and evidence of a new 4,500ft runway on Utagal. The map shows two seaplane taxiways (left) sheltered by the string of smaller atolls.

Below Right: Prior to the U.S. invasion in June 1944, Saipan was extensively photographed. This print, dated February 22, shows Garapan town and Tanapag Harbor and seaplane base at far left.

the lightweight Japanese fighters. Also highly favored for its twin-engined reliability, the P-38 became the fighter most desired by commanders in the Pacific. Several of the top U.S. air aces of the war flew P-38s in the Pacific.

BOUGAINVILLE AND TARAWA

On November 1, 1943, the Allies again took the Japanese by surprise by landing on southern Bougainville. Following large-scale air attacks that neutralized the Japanese airfields on nearby Shortland Island, this ambitious operation by the 3rd Marine Division was ultimately seen as wasteful if not actually unnecessary. A strong defensive perimeter was, nevertheless, established, and although the nature of Bougainville's terrain prevented much movement inland, the enemy was obliged to stay put.

Unable to launch a counter-attack until March 8, 1944, the Japanese ultimately lost 5,500 men of the 6th Division trying to destroy the well fortified beach-head. Thereafter, they all but ignored the defenders, then comprising the American and 37th Divisions which had relieved the Marines. Having tied down and cut off 37,000 Japanese troops of the Seventeenth Army, four Australian militia brigades set about hunting them down, starting in October 1944. The campaign did not end until August 1945 with the surrender of no less than 23,500 Japanese troops.

On November 12, the Japanese made a partial withdrawal from the isolated garrison at Rabaul on New Britain, which had been pounded ceaselessly by Allied aircraft. Then, on November 19, U.S. warships fired the last rounds of a massive pre-invasion bombardment at Tarawa, the curtain raiser to the first operation to forcibly eject the Japanese from an island base.

By landing on Tarawa, a tiny atoll in the Gilbert Islands, the U.S. came up against the kind of tenacious enemy resistance that would, in varying degrees, mark all such operations in the future. Admiral Turner's 5th Amphibious Force, comprising nearly 7,000 men of the U.S. Army's 27th Division, would assault Butaritari on Makin, while about 18,000 Marines of the 2nd Division had Betio Island, Tarawa as their objective. There was hardly any interference to the U.S. assault force from the IJN as Admiral Koga was occupied with a naval operation at

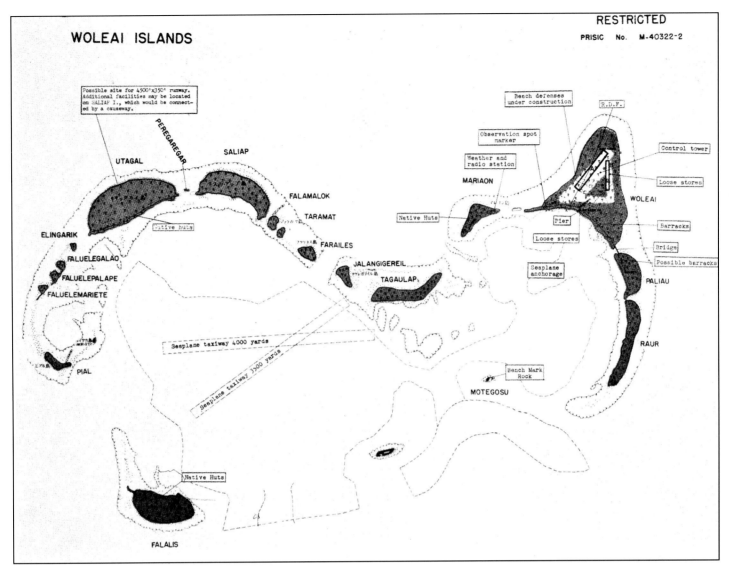

RESTRICTED

PRISIC No. M-40322-2

WOLEAI ISLANDS

Possible site for 4500'x350' runway. Additional facilities may be located on SALIAP I., which would be connected by a causeway.

PEREGAREGAR

UTAGAL

SALIAP

FALAMALOK

TARAMAT

Native huts

FARAILES

ELINGARIK

FALUELEGALAO

FALUELEPALAPE

JALANGIGEREIL

FALUELEMARIETE

TAGAULAP

PIAL

Seaplane taxiway 4000 yards

Seaplane taxiway 3500 yards

Bench Mark Rock

MOTEGOSU

Beach defenses under construction

R.D.F.

Observation spot marker

Control tower

Weather and radio station

Loose stores

MARIAON

WOLEAI

Native Huts

Pier

Barracks

Loose stores

Bridge

Possible barracks

Seaplane anchorage

PALIAU

RAUR

Native Huts

FALALIS

TANAPAG HARBOR

SEAPLANE BASE

MAIN WHARF

GARAPAN

MUTCHO POINT

N

RESTRICTED
JICPOA

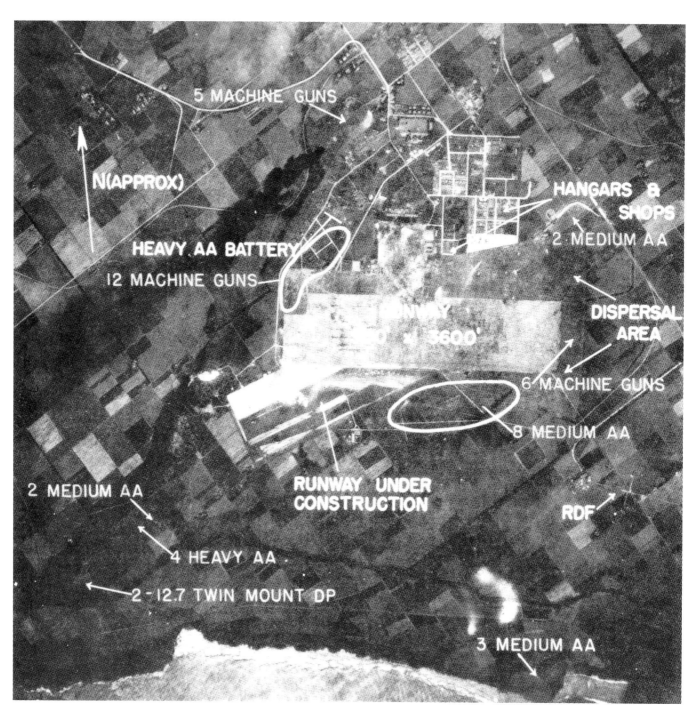

Above: A primary U.S. target on Saipan was Aslito airfield. It was, as can be seen, well defended with heavy, medium and light AAA guns as well as machine guns covering all approaches.

Rabaul, and he thus passed up the long-awaited fleet engagement with the Americans.

Air strikes and a two-hour naval bombardment preceded the Makin landings on November 20. Butaritari was defended by a garrison of some 800 Japanese, who fought for three days, taking 350 casualties. The Americans fared worse with 860 casualties, 644 of them as a result of the sinking of the escort carrier *Liscombe Bay* by the submarine *I-175* on November 24.

At Tarawa, where the main objective was Betio airfield, a much more in-depth defense confronted General Holland Smith's Marines. As well as adverse tides, which hampered the landing boats, the Marines had to contend with log and concrete obstacles, barbed wire, bunkers, and tunnels, all swept by withering enemy fire. Artillery support was also available to the 4,800 defenders of the island, who were commanded by Rear-Adm. Keiji Shibasaki. Defenses at the landing points, designated as Beach Red 1, 2, and 3, were tackled by amphtracs and Sherman tanks, and the fighting to establish a secure beach-head was bitter. When they could get inland, the Americans found less opposition, but in three days of murderous combat the Marines suffered 3,300 casualties while having to wipe out the Japanese almost to the last man. No quarter, hand-to-hand combat finished a nightmare battle that stamped itself indelibly on the minds of those who survived it.

Smith was far from convinced that "Bloody Tarawa" was worth the cost, but it did secure vital airfields. The Marines also gained valuable practical experience of the requirements of future amphibious operations. The sobering lesson, that the enemy was willing to die rather than surrender, was well learned. It would soon be put to an even more severe test.

In order to take the war to the Japanese the U.S. planned and carried out a series of raids into the Pacific; to actually wrest back the most important areas captured by the enemy would take time and careful planning to determine which of these was the most important to their own operations, as well as those that would tear major holes in the Japanese outer defensive perimeter. Airfields and anchorages were usually the deciding factor. Assaulting certain bases which were heavily defended but did not have geographical features suitable for bases would incur needless casualties for little tactical gain. Consequently the U.S. Joint Chiefs, as part of

their strategy for the future prosecution of the war, opted to contain and bypass locations such as Rabaul which would be left, in Douglas MacArthur's words, "To wither on the vine."

During 1943 American war resources had been steadily building up; by the spring the first of the superb "Fletcher" class destroyers had made its action debut at Guadalcanal, and new vessels were coming off the slipways at a steady rate. Nine new carriers, including the first vessels of the much more effective "Essex" class, able to carry up to 100 aircraft, were commissioned between December 31, 1942, and mid-June 1943.

If the U.S. Navy lacked anything at that point it was replacements for some of the "big guns" lost at Pearl Harbor. While the battleship was fast relinquishing its place as the capital ship of the world's navies to the aircraft carrier, the American heavy ships were much used in the

Below: Saipan was well defended by the Japanese to no avail. A 75mm Type 94 Army field gun was one of many knocked out by the U.S. invasion, its shield having been pierced by .50-caliber rounds.

Pacific, particularly in pre-invasion "softening up" bombardment of enemy-held shores. Older vessels, those only damaged and even sunk in shallow water on December 7, were raised, refitted and returned to action. The USS *Iowa*, named vessel of the last class of U.S. battleships to be commissioned, would join the fleet early in 1944.

The United States was initially obliged to rely on cruisers, several of which had been lost in the early campaigns in the southwest Pacific. Japan had managed to kept her pre-war, treaty-breaking cruiser-building program secret, this enabling the IJN to deploy them as an integral part of most early war actions.

After taking Guadalcanal, New Guinea, Bougainville, and the Gilberts, phase five of the American drive across the central Pacific was to capture the Mariana islands, which formed part of Micronesia.

THE MARIANAS

A major step along the road back across the central Pacific was to secure the main islands of Micronesia—Guam, Tinian, and Saipan in the Marianas group—as a major base complex for long-range heavy bombers. The U.S. Navy carried out an initial carrier raid on the Marianas on February 22, 1944. There followed an established pattern of initial air attacks of varying intensity, depending on the size of target and the known strength of the defenses. Air strikes also obtained an up to the minute picture of the defenses, which were naturally subject to change. Aerial photography and crew observation would confirm such valuable details as new fortifications and any fresh airfield activity, particularly runway extension work, additional revetments, and increased AAA defense. A seaborne bombardment would immediately precede the amphibious landings to knock out most visible defensive positions.

For the invasion of the Marianas, which began on June 15, 1944, Mark Mitscher's 5th Fleet included 15 carriers, 7 battleships, 21 cruisers, and 69 destroyers. In addition there were 28 submarines to provide long-range, outer perimeter cover. Closer to the objectives, 11 escort carriers would provide fleet defense and close air support for the invading troops.

Below Right: Truk was the Japanese Navy's main base until 1943 when it was abandoned after extensive attack by the U.S. Navy. A series of post-strike photos included a view of what appears to be the knocked-out radio station.

Below: U.S. forces learned the difficult art of taking well-defended islands and atolls at Tarawa in late 1943. Low strung trip wires set just inshore of the waterline were part of a nest of enemy beach defenses.

The Marianas would be attacked in the order Saipan, Tinian, and then Guam. On June 15, the assault commenced. Marines of the 2nd and 4th Divisions and the Army's 27th Infantry Division were put ashore on Saipan. The landings were hardly unopposed; 8,000 Marines went ashore in the first wave of the assault and by nightfall, despite heavy casualties, about 20,000 troops had landed and established a five-mile long beach-head. Pinned down on the beaches, the Marines awaited the landing of their tanks to stop dangerous Japanese counter-attacks.

When the Marines captured Mount Tapotchau on June 27, it was only a matter of time before the enemy finally succumbed. Even so, Marines and Army infantry alike were obliged to continue fighting for the heart of Saipan, with the desperate enemy expending thousands of troops in pointless Banzai charges. The island was finally secured on July 9 at a cost of 24,000 enemy dead and 3,426 U.S. casualties.

Admiral Soemu Toyoda, in command of the Combined Fleet after Koga's death in service, ordered Vice-Adm. Jisaburo Ozawa's Mobile Fleet to intercept Mitscher's ships. He had nine carriers under his command with a total of about 440 aircraft embarked. Added to this was the strength of the Marianas-based 61st Air Flotilla which had previously been reported as having around 630 aircraft. Although this figure

had been reduced, the Japanese clearly enjoyed a numerical air superiority. This was not to prove decisive, as the air groups could no longer boast aircrew of the same caliber as those who had begun the war. By contrast the U.S. aviators were well trained and motivated, and flew excellent aircraft.

On August 31, 1943, a new American fighter, the Grumman F6F Hellcat, had made its combat debut in the hands of Navy squadron VF-5. Then flying from *Yorktown* as part of TF-15, the Hellcat pilots opened their score on October 5. That was the start of an incredible run of victories that would make the F6F the scourge of the Japanese air forces and, in terms of the number of pilots who became aces while flying it, the war's most successful combat aircraft. The Hellcat would play a particularly important role in the Marianas battles as we shall see.

Five battleships and 13 cruisers, plus destroyers, completed one of the largest Japanese battle groups ever to put to sea. The U.S. submarine screen soon detected this force and warned Spruance, who delayed capture of the Marianas in favor of securing his forces from IJN attack. Anticipating that the Japanese ships would attack from two directions, and adopting extreme caution, Spruance postponed the landing on Guam (scheduled for June 18) and sent Mitscher to intercept the enemy at a point about

N.OB2/5 PROB. HIT ON TRUK RADIO.

Right: For all its sophisticated casevac arrangements during the Pacific war, the U.S. occasionally found that the huge numbers of men involved tested the methods that had to be used. Getting the badly wounded up ship gangways from amphtracs was one of the challenges that had to be overcome.

160 miles west of the islands. Battle commenced the following day when a U.S. submarine torpedoed two carriers, the Pearl Harbor veteran *Shokaku* and the *Taiho*, Ozawa's flagship which blew up and sank that afternoon.

Four separate carrier strikes were launched by the Japanese on June 19, Ozawa sending 326 aircraft to destroy the U.S. carriers. It was they who were destroyed—the "Marianas Turkey Shoot" was on.

Intercepted by hordes of Hellcats, the enemy aircraft fell blazing into the ocean one after another; those that evaded the CAP faced the red hot barrels of thousands of naval guns. It was not only the IJN dive and torpedo bombers that were decimated. Japanese fighters fared little better as the Hellcat was more than a match for the now outclassed Zero. For placing a single bomb on an American ship the Japanese paid the price of 240 aircraft against 29 American, a single-day loss ratio that no force could sustain.

American air strikes also whittled down the Japanese fleet. Chasing Ozawa's carriers westward, Mitscher launched a long-range strike on June 20 which caught and sank the carrier *Hiyo* and damaged other vessels. The losses, however, were not one-sided; by the time the battle was over, the long pursuit to find the ships saw darkness falling. The U.S. carrier aircraft made their

way home, many with their fuel tanks fast running dry. Soon Helldivers, Avengers, and Hellcats began to ditch, and distress calls filled the airwaves. Those crews that made it back to the carriers had to land with low fuel on darkened decks. As they started, so did the accidents. Mitscher, abandoning security to save his airmen, ordered the fleet to, "Turn on the lights." His bold action that night saved many flyers from, at least, a soaking in a dark, cold ocean.

The invasion of Guam, which had been preceded by two weeks of bombardment by U.S. battleships and cruisers, finally took place on July 21. Using three divisions—the 3rd Marine Division, the 1st Marine Brigade, and the 77th Infantry Division—to prevent the casualties suffered on Saipan, Maj-Gen. Roy Geiger's troops found that many fortified positions had been pulverized by naval shells, but that many Japanese soldiers remained unharmed in numerous caves and bunkers.

Destroying one strongpoint after another as they made their way laboriously inland, the Americans also fended off night Banzai charges. The arrival of Army P-47s on Saipan, a few miles from Guam's combat areas, on June 22 helped the ground troops mop up stubborn pockets of resistance.

Declared secure by August 8, Guam's new tenants had to contend with Japanese snipers until the end of the war—and some of these, cut off from the outside world, did not "surrender" until the 1970s.

While the battle for Guam continued, Tinian's northwestern beaches were chosen as the landing points for the 2nd and 4th Marine Divisions on July 24. Securing the third main island in the Marianas proved far less costly than its neighbors, the battle ending with 389 men killed and 1,816 wounded. Operating quickly and efficiently, the Marines had cleared Tinian by August 1.

While the troops completed their operations ashore, the Navy took steps to prevent the enemy attacking the U.S. assault forces with fresh aircraft from Japan staging through Iwo Jima. Carrier strikes on the Bonin and Volcano Islands continued the spiraling attrition rate.

The disastrous battle for the Marianas had a far-reaching effect on Japan. With the nation's seapower all but broken, the Tojo war cabinet resigned en masse on July 18; the new cabinet was charged with what was termed at the time as "fundamental reconsideration" of the problems of continuing the war.

The point of securing the Marianas was to create bomber bases, and once the fighting had died down the Seabees did just that. Equipped with graders and bulldozers, these military construction engineers rapidly transformed the modest Japanese airstrips into bases large enough to accommodate B-29s. They very rapidly had runways, aircraft hardstandings, acres of living quarters, administrative buildings, transportation areas, and fuel and bomb dumps. To complete the work as quickly as possible, the islanders themselves were recruited to aid the U.S. war effort. To make enough hardcore to pave the runways, crushing plants were built to break up coral which was then trucked to the required area and laid in place. On October 12, 1944, four months after the first amphibious landings, the first B-29 touched down on Saipan.

Below: C-47s cruise over the drop zone in New Guinea's Markham Valley on September 5, 1943. An unopposed landing by the 503rd Parachute Regiment enabled an airfield to be rapidly built at Nadzab.

Bottom: Smoke drifts over the Markham Valley to mask the activities of the U.S. paratroops in the September 1943 operation to secure the area and build an airfield. A suitable sight at Nadzab was opened to traffic the following day.

59

BURMA BATTLEGROUND

4. THE JAPANESE THRUST TOWARD INDIA

BURMA

The huge areas of southeast Asia invaded by the Japanese in 1941–42 included the resource-rich territory of Burma. With that country secured, it was part of the long-range Japanese war plan to ultimately push through Imphal and launch an invasion of India. Burma was garrisoned by British troops—rarely more than two army battalions but, from 1941, with the support of local Burmese. Reinforcements had also been sent from India before the war, giving the commander in Burma, Lt-Gen. Sir Thomas Hutton, a nominal two divisions, the 1st Burma and the 17th Indian. However, as became evident elsewhere, these forces were poorly equipped and far from fully trained. RAF airpower available to Hutton was also severely rationed.

Consequently, when the Japanese attacked in December 1941, they were quickly able to threaten not just British forces locally, but Britain's overall control of Burma.

The Imperial Army crossed into Burma from Siam with one of its first objectives the occupa-tion of Victorial Point, on the west side of the Kra Isthmus. By January 1942 Japanese troops were in a position to launch a full-scale offensive. The advance began on the 15th, a thrust towards Moulmein on the eastern bank of the Salween River securing all three airfields on the Tenasserin coast. Using these bases, bombing raids with fighter escort could be mounted against Rangoon. They were opposed by the RAF and a single squadron of P-40 Warhawks of the American Volunteer Group, the famed "Flying Tigers." These fighters, when they could get airborne in time, usually ensured that bomber operations by the Japanese were not conducted without cost.

The problem for the British was that supplies for Burma were channeled through the vulnerable port of Rangoon, but Hutton concentrated on defending southern Burma in the hope that the Japanese Fifteenth Army could be held. This

Below: Airpower dominated the Burma front and among the types used by the RAF was the P-47 Thunderbolt, one of the war's most effective fighter-bombers. These Thunderbolts are taxying past Hurricanes, the fighter they generally replaced.

Top: The Fourteenth Army's "secret weapon" to win the Burma ground war was supply by air. RAF Dakotas parachuted all manner of supplies to troops cut off from any other means of obtaining the sustenance of war.

Above: Japanese railheads were always important targets for Allied bombers.

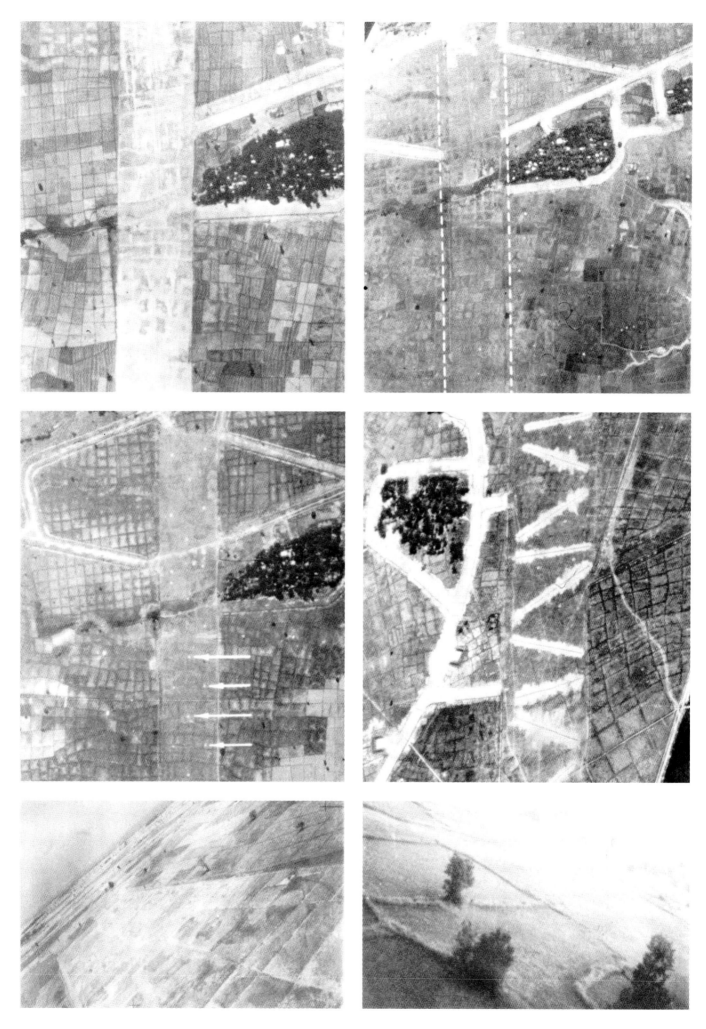

Left to Right, Top to Bottom
A serviceable strip yet to be rolled
An overgrown strip rendered unserviceable by monsoon rains.
Aerial cameras pick out demolition pits dug along the strip.
Trenches across the strip deny any immediate use by Allied aircraft.
Two oblique views of airstrips laid over paddy fields, highlighting their deceptive surface.

hope was dashed as the Japanese moved quickly to encircle Allied units. By February 11 they had established a bridgehead west of the Salween. The 17th Indian Division withdrew to avoid encirclement, but a line on the Bilin River was only lightly held and a further withdrawal, to the Sittang, had to be made. The Sittang was the last major obstacle to the Japanese advance on Rangoon. Cut off by a blown bridge, many Indian troops were trapped on the east bank and killed both by enemy troops and air attack.

Hutton's advice that Rangoon should now be evacuated was countermanded by Wavell, awaiting reinforcements which he knew were en route. Wavell made some command changes, including the replacement of Hutton with Sir Harold Alexander. The latter was ordered to hold Rangoon as long as possible, but by March 5, the Japanese were making for the Irrawaddy, threatening to cut off the British and Indian troops.

Meanwhile, the expected reinforcements, the 7th Armoured Brigade and the 17th Indian Divison, had arrived, and these were positioned to provide flank and rearguard cover while the Chinese Fifth and Sixth Armies, sent by Chiang Kai-shek, undertook to hold the eastern flank at Toungoo and in the Shan States. Alexander attempted to impede the enemy at Prome without success, and it became clear that all southern Burma would have to be abandoned to the Japanese.

Securing the port facilities of Rangoon was a major boost to the Japanese supply position, by then almost as dire as that of the British, who now faced a long retreat toward India. Early in May British forces had also to withdrew from Mandalay and Irrawaddy, the retreat culminating in a crossing of the Burma-India frontier on the 15th. The Japanese fortified their newly-won positions in Burma and, deploying two new divisions, the 18th and 56th, harassed the retreat, which became the longest in British military history. Nearly a thousand miles had been covered by the time the Allied troops crossed the Chindwin River on May 20, 1942.

One bright spot in the otherwise disastrous first Burma campaign had been Burcorps. An abbreviation of Burma Corps, the force comprised the 17th Indian Division, 7th Armoured Brigade, 1st Burma Division, and support troops under the commend of Lt-Gen. William J "Bill"

Below: Merrill's Marauders had secured Myitkyina airfield by May 17, 1944—the day the Japanese carried out an air raid. One man wields a .50in machine gun, while another aims his Thompson at an enemy aircraft which was probably bent on strafing the C-47 visible at right.

Slim, who would later lead the Fourteenth Army's drive to retake Burma. Burcorps had fought well, and although the campaign was lost, it had provided invaluable experience of enemy tactics, the demanding requirements of jungle fighting, and the vital need for a reliable supply organization.

For the Chinese, the loss of Burma effectively isolated her from any other supply route except the Allied air corridor over the Himalayas, known as the "Hump." Despite repeated Japanese attempts to close it, the notorious Burma road remained open.

In the meantime the Japanese maintained their offensive elsewhere. Operations against the islands of the so-called Malay Barrier, which included Sumatra, Java, and the Dutch East Indies, succeeded in all but swamping thinly-spread Dutch, British, Indian, and Australian forces. Areas such as that of British Borneo were simply too large to hold against a determined foe and the high command plumped for one place—Kuching in Western Sarawak.

On May 7, as we have seen earlier, the day after the final fall of the Philippines, the U.S. Navy clashed with the Japanese fleet for the first time in the Coral Sea, the ensuing action resulting in the sinking of the carrier *Shoho*. Despite this setback at sea, Japanese war plans for land campaigns during this period appeared to possess their own momentum; ignoring the fact that they were inevitably spreading their forces somewhat thinly, they sortied against still weak Allied opposition and, in most cases, quickly won the day. Likewise thrusting outward from their bases at Rabaul and Truk, the Japanese admirals followed operational orders, selecting the most effective routings from a number of operational options, should Allied reaction force changes of plan.

7   159/986. 10 JUL 45. F.5.//6000. → 7×500. 4×250 T.I.
000. 12.3L "B" F/o HAYCOCK. "K" BANKOK.

However, with every new conquest, the Japanese committed themselves to an ever-widening war. In China the campaign had become a series of limited offensives with a constant ebb and flow. Having learned from early setbacks, the Chinese were capable of inflicting casualties on the invaders. Policing the country tied up thousands of Japanese troops, and localized battles saw territory change hands more than once. With Allied help, both in the form of direct supplies to Chiang Kai-shek and the stationing of USAAF combat units in the country, the Japanese were often unable to fully exploit gains.

Having managed to keep the Burma Road open despite constant attack from the Japanese, the Allies maintained a tenuous supply link with China from India. Airpower was the real key to keeping the Chinese supplied, and the USAAF's air route over the Hump was ultimately to prove decisive in defeating the enemy.

REVIVAL IN INDIA

After the early war defeats in Malaya and Burma, the British reorganized in India to the extent that, by 1943, counter-offensive operations against the Japanese could be undertaken with a reasonable chance of success. Aerial reconnaissance gathered comprehensive data on the often featureless jungle areas over which future campaigns would have to be fought, and whereas the Far East remained somewhat lower down the list of theater priority in terms of equipment and supplies than the forces in situ would have liked, the RAF continued its offensive as improved aircraft arrived. Very active over Burma were types such as the Vultee Vengeance dive bomber, the B-24 Liberator, and Bristol Beaufighter. Dubbed the "Whispering Death" by the harassed Japanese, the "Beau" became the scourge of enemy supply lines,

Above: Also defending Myitkyina by May 17, 1944, were artillery positions manned by the Chinese. Lt-Gen. Stillwell had several Chinese armies helping to defeat the Japanese in Burma.

particularly the railways. Bombing and strafing trains, rolling stock and bridges as well as road and river traffic, the air force made Japanese occupancy of many areas increasingly difficult

A simple weapon that proved very effective against the Burmese railway system was the spike bomb. Dropped at very low level, most frequently by RAF Liberators and U.S. Mitchells, these otherwise conventional HE bombs could bore into the soft track bed before exploding and tearing up the sleepers and rails for yards around.

SEAC ESTABLISHED

From mid-1943 British forces in India were under the stewardship of General Sir Claude Auchinleck, who succeeded Wavell in June. That autumn, firm plans for major new offensives took a step nearer implementation. A fresh headquarters structure to direct the recapture of Burma and Malaya was established—as Southeast Asia Command (SEAC)—in October. Under the command of Vice-Adm. Lord Louis Mountbatten, SEAC took responsibility for all land, sea, and air forces in the Indian Ocean, the Bay of Bengal, and surrounding areas.

To direct a U.S. involvement in Burma Lt-Gen. Joseph "Vinegar Joe" Stilwell became Mountbatten's second in command.

SEAC's Fourteenth Army, comprising IV and IX Corps, was under Lt-Gen. "Bill" Slim, who commanded about one million men including British, Indian, Gurkha, Burmese, and African troops. Apart from the key factor of utilizing U.S. transport aircraft, the command's air assets including the long-range Strategic Air Force equipped with RAF Liberator squadrons, while fighter and medium bomber elements combined RAF and American units. Some of the former re-equipped with the P-47 Thunderbolt, a type new to British squadrons. These heavily armed fighter-bombers were highly effective at destroying a variety of Japanese ground targets, air combat becoming something of a rarity over Burma as the enemy progressively withdrew his airpower to other areas. Not having to worry unduly

Above Right: Stationary tank fire from a paddyfield in the Rasabil area of Burma ranging in on Japanese ridge positions. Using 75mm HE shells and machine gun fire, the tanks, usually firing direct, could hit targets over ranges of 300 to 600 yards. Hilltop observation points assisted when targets were obscured by undergrowth.

Center Right: During January and February 1944 the Arakan was the scene of the first tank actions in Burma. It wasn't ideal ground for armored warfare. Stretches of flat paddy broken by razorback ridges thickly covered by secondary undergrowth made ideal concealment for enemy troops.

Right: Allied supplies being moved through the Ngakyedauk Pass in Burma's Arakan region.

about enemy air activity was a great relief to Allied aircrew in planning "the road back."

In January 1944, IV Corps under Lt-Gen. Geoffrey Scoones made a limited advance against Japanese positions in the Imphal area west of the Chindwin, while XV Corps (Lt-Gen. Philip Christison) pushed towards Buthidaung and Maungdaw in the Arakan. A concurrent Chindit insertion, Operation "Thursday," saw about 9,000 men positioned behind enemy lines.

Japanese strength was not only found to be much greater than had been anticipated; Allied troops ran into an offensive by the 55th Division of the Japanese Twenty-eighth Army as it pushed into the Arakan. This move was part of the Operation "Ha-Go" plan of 1942 which had been postponed for about a year due to troop transfers to the South Pacific. It called for the Fifteenth Army under Lt-Gen. Renya Mutaguchi with units of the 18th, 33rd, and 55th Divisions, to take Imphal, Kohima, Ledo, and other locations along the India-Burma border. During 1943 the Japanese had been forced into a position similar to that of the Allies, albeit for a different reason, and had seen little action.

Anticipating a major British offensive early in 1944, Tokyo decreed that every effort should be made to prevent it because British success would ultimately threaten the Japanese hold on Indo-China and Siam. The additional presence of Chindits behind Japanese lines gave rise to grave doubts that Burma could be held, but the original "Ha-Go" plan, with its primary objective as Imphal, went ahead virtually unchanged. If they captured Imphal, the Japanese planned to take Kohima and destroy Allied airfields and communications between north Assam and China.

Had Slim been forced to commit his reserves as the Japanese hoped, then Operation "U-Go," the advance to Imphal and Kohima, would have been far less of a risk—and when they managed to surround the 7th Indian Division, the initial offensive by the Japanese appeared to be succeeding. However, Slim, promising air supply of the Indian troops, persuaded them to hold firm in the "Admin Box" at Sunzweya until three divisions could reach them. The 7th Division was relieved and the victory revitalized the Allied campaign to win back all of Burma.

Slim anticipated that the Japanese would renew the offensive. They did so on March 15, and Slim drew them back towards the Imphal plain where the 17th and 20th Divisions would make a stand. Then IV Corps, with strong armored support, threw a steel ring around Imphal. This battle, which was to last until June 22, saw the Japanese 15th and 31st Divisions suffer a major defeat. In retreat, ill-equipped and starving through lack of supplies, the Japanese suffered appalling casualties.

In late April the Japanese 31st Division had attacked Kohima in force, and a bloody, protracted battle ensued. For 12 days the garrison held out until relieved, and although much hard fighting still lay ahead, by June 3 the Japanese had also begun to retreat on this sector of the Burma front.

At the end of what was SEAC's major campaign in the Far East, the Japanese 15th Division had suffered 53,000 casualties from its original strength of 85,000 men. The victory, speeded by the participation of Chinese divisions of Stilwell's Northern Combat Area Command and Merrill's Marauders operating along the Salween, made possible the total reconquest of Burma.

Building on Fourteenth Army's success, in November 1944 Mountbatten launched Operational "Capital" to completely secure Burma. This land invasion was not allowed, as previously, to be interrupted by the monsoon, and XXXIII Corps (Lt-Gen. Montagu Stopford) and the 11th East African Division made good progress, the enemy being pushed across the Chindwin and falling back on the Irrawaddy. When he found the Japanese retreating across the river, Slim reacted by sending the 7th Indian Division to cross at Nyaungi as an outflanking move. The Japanese defended their main supply base at Meiktila with some vigor, but this fell to a flying column of Stopford's armor on March 3.

As Slim had foreseen, the excellent air resupply service became the key to the Allies holding onto the base. Both the 19th Division and XXXIII Corps had fought their way across the Irrawaddy by February 12, 1945, and IV Corps had an easier time in its crossing. These moves effectively trapped the Japanese Fifteenth and Thirty-third Armies, cutting them off from their bases in southern Burma. On top of this, the enemy could not maintain communications with its Twenty-eighth Army.

March saw Mandalay fall to XXXIII Corps, which had linked up with IV Corps by the end of that month. The trapped Japanese armies began to disintegrate to the point where they posed no further major threat to Allied operations in that area.

Racing to reach Rangoon before the monsoon made operations difficult if not impossible, Fourteenth Army spearheads were halted at Pegu, a mere 50 miles from the Burmese capital as the weather broke. As a result Operation "Dracula" was executed, and amphibious forces, backed up by paratroops, entered the city, only to find that the Japanese had fled.

Now fighting a desperate rearguard action, the Japanese attempted to evacuate their depleted armies from Burma by way of the Sittang valley into Siam and Malaya. Any such regrouping in those countries had to stopped, and Allied troops hunted down and eventually rounded up some 16,000 enemy troops.

Bill Slim's victory in Burma was crowned by the unopposed Allied entry into Malaya—Operation "Zipper," the plan to take Singapore, being curtailed by the Japanese surrender.

Above Right: By 1944 the Allies in Burma could afford to move in the open in daylight, a luxury increasingly denied to the Japanese who were forced to conceal vulnerable locomotives from air attack by shelters such as this.

Center Right: Reconnaissance pin-pointed the position of locomotive shelters for subsequent destruction.

Right: Larger scale targets posed problems for Allied airmen as this vertical of Mandalay shows—was the large camp an enemy-held target area or a PoW camp?

MACARTHUR RETURNS

5. RETAKING PELELIEU, LEYTE, AND THE PHILIPPINES

BACKGROUND

As seen earlier, the final abandonment of the Philippines came with the surrender of Corregidor in April 1942, when the United States relinquished one of its major bases. Despite the loss of his command, Douglas MacArthur left with a stirring pledge—"I shall return"—giving some hope to the Filipino population, who faced a grim period under Japanese occupation. The general returned home to what amounted to a hero's welcome before going to Australia where the U.S. established a forward area base, notwithstanding the enemy threat to the country when Darwin was bombed.

PELELIEU

From the relative security of Australia, a few last air raids on the Philippines were made in April 1942, before the Japanese occupation was complete. Thereafter MacArthur pressed for the re-taking of the Philippines at the earliest opportunity, a move resisted by the U.S. Navy until such a time when such a gigantic undertaking could be sure of success. The Navy's realistic view was that, as only four of the thousands of islands that constituted the Philippines had any military value, the operation could easily have been postponed indefinitely. The political advantage of MacArthur leading the forces who would retake the islands was not, however, lost on Roosevelt, although it was not until the autumn of 1944 that the invasion went ahead.

As a curtain-raiser to invading the Philippines the U.S. 31st Division occupied Morotai on September 15. This landing was unopposed, unlike the assault on Pelelieu in the Palau Islands, lying on the western edge of the Carolines which began that same day. The 1st

Below: U.S. power at sea grew quickly to the point where a fleet could deploy multiple carriers for a single operation. Nine are visible in this view.

Above: Escort carrier USS *Lunga Point* took part in the Lingayen Gulf action, this bow view showing her disruptive camouflage pattern.

Marine Division under General Rupertus stormed ashore to be met with heavy fire from Japanese troops dug into caves. Having used conventional small arms and machine guns, the Marines brought up flamethrowers to clear the enemy more quickly. This grisly form of warfare proved one of the most effective weapons in dealing with well dug in soldiers who stubbornly resisted all other inducements to surrender. Many Japanese chose to be burned alive rather than give up; others indulged in suicidal charges straight onto the American guns.

Four weeks into the fighting and Peleliéu threatened to become another Tarawa; in that period 1,121 Marines were killed. It was only a matter of time before the tenacious Marines prevailed, however, and on November 25 the battle ended when the last remnants of an enemy garrison of 5,300 men had been eliminated at a cost of 1,950 American lives.

LEYTE

In October 1944 a Northern Attack Force under Rear-Adm. Daniel Barbey was assembled to take Leyte and Mindoro as initial objectives. By combining Barbey's force with a Southern Attack Force led by Vice-Adm. Theodore Wilkinson, the Philippine invasion force became a 500-ship fleet which would land 20,000 combat troops of the U.S. Sixth Army.

To circumvent Japanese air power based on Formosa from attacking the U.S. fleet, large scale air strikes were mounted between October 10 and 16, these resulting in huge dogfights in which the Japanese lost heavily. Desperately the IJN sent reinforcements of carrier aircraft in a vain attempt to offset the staggering destruction of some 500 machines in the air and on the ground.

The U.S. forces certainly did not underestimate the likely scale of the operation to recapture the Philippines; the risk was underscored by the fact that Halsey's fast carriers could only be indirectly committed, as a major IJN fleet challenge to the landings was anticipated. Instead, MacArthur would have at his disposal 18 Third Fleet escort carriers plus the long rifles of Admiral Jesse Oldendorf's battleship bombardment force. An additional hazard to the landing was Japanese land-based airpower (the Fourth Air Army) which was to be used in conjunction with action by the Combined Fleet in executing

the SHO-I plan. Even though many Japanese aircraft had been destroyed before the assault began, no U.S. commander fooled himself that more would not appear over his ships as soon as the operation began.

The Japanese realized that they had to concentrate their forces on Leyte, which was 100 miles long by a maximum of 40 miles wide. If they were to retain the Philippines, the island had to be held—there was no question of trying to maintain garrisons in other areas. Consequently, Lt-Gen. Tomoyuki Yamashita deployed his Fourteenth Area Army, about ten infantry divisions, and an armored division, in the mountainous and inhospitable terrain that made up most of Leyte. It was ideal for defense, the only flat area lying to the west and northeast wherein lay the main U.S. objectives, the airfields at Dulag and Tacloban.

The invasion began on October 20, 1944, when the U.S. XXIV Corps (the 7th and 96th Army Divisions) landed near Dulag and X Corps (1st Cavalry and 24th Division) was put ashore three miles from Tacloban. To help the troops hold their positions, the IJN immediately launched powerful fleet elements which aimed to destroy the ships of the American landing force at their most vulnerable. Three massive fleets were deployed: Admiral Ozawa's Northern Force of six carriers, Admiral Kurita's Central Force—without carriers but with five battleships including both the world's largest warships, the *Musashi* and *Yamato*—and Vice-Adm.

Nishimura's Southern Force, the core of which was two battleships and a heavy cruiser.

Under a typically elaborate Japanese plan, Ozawa was to draw Halsey's carriers off while the Central and Southern Forces decimated the invasion fleet. On October 24, Japanese bombers scored an early success by sinking the carrier *Princeton*. Halsey's air groups responded with vigor against the Central Force and sank the *Musashi*.

Halsey, having sighted Kurita and noted the lack of carriers, made a controversial decision to withdraw his fleet carriers in the hope that the enemy would pursue and suffer further casualties. This plan only partially succeeded—as did that put into operation by Admiral Nishimura. Running into accurate battleship shelling, he pulled away with the battleship *Yamashiro* a floating wreck from aerial bombing and the cruiser *Mogami* badly damaged.

On the 27th Kurita, ordered back into San Bernardino Strait to attack the U.S. transports, opened fire on Admiral Clifton Sprague's six escort carriers patrolling off Samur. The carriers, frantically making smoke to shield themselves, steamed south with all speed to avoid the deluge of fire suddenly raining down on them, but the Japanese shells soon turned the CVE *Gambier Bay* into a blazing hulk. She was abandoned as the Japanese themselves came under attack from aircraft based aboard the remaining Jeep carriers.

Poor ship recognition by the Japanese blunted what could have been a major victory at Leyte

Above Left: Multiple frames of camera gun film from the F6F Hellcat flown by Ensign R.E. Pfeifer, who downed a "Zeke" over the west coast of Luzon on January 5, 1945.

Left: Off the Philippines in January 1945 aircraft from the USS *Savo Island* spotted a submerged submarine, assumed to be Japanese, off the town of Damortis in Lingayen Gulf. It is just visible at the bottom of the photograph.

Right: Identified as hostile, the Japanese submarine was flushed out and apparently sunk by aircraft from the escort carrier.

Top: A minesweeping unit led by YMS-48 coming under enemy shore fire off Corregidor on February 14, 1945.

Above: Major sea actions off the Philippines were decisive for the United States' forces, the outcome allowing landings in Lingayen Gulf to proceed without disruption from.

Far Right: The acute need for minesweepers around Corregidor was starkly illustrated when LMS-169 blew up in Mariveles Harbor on February 12, 1945.

Right: The long struggle to retake the Philippines included large-scale troop landings on Mindanao.

Gulf; by mistaking the carrier covering force of destroyers for cruisers, Kurita hesitated. So violent was the destroyers' attack on his ships that he decided to withdraw, but not before sinking the *Johnston* and *Hoel*.

Air attacks finally persuaded Kurita to break off and he abandoned prematurely any further chance to wreak great destruction on the invasion transports off Leyte, for the Japanese admiral was unaware of how desperate a situation the engagement was for Sprague's escort force. The American admiral was not about to reveal that fact, and at one point the escort carrier air groups were pitted against the might of the isolated and fleeing *Yamato*, their Wildcat fighters cheekily strafing the superstructure of the behemoth and inflicting some damage.

Losses in the Battle of Leyte Gulf finally broke the back of the Combined Fleet. Halsey, pursued north (as he had planned), turned on the Japanese and accounted for all four of Ozawa's carriers. With one superbattleship also down, two cruisers badly damaged, and smaller ships lost, the Japanese had but one last throw—the kamikazes. First encountered in numbers by the Americans during this battle, the suicide attacks were aimed at the carriers of the Third Fleet.

BATTLE FOR THE PHILIPPINES

While the amphibious invasion of the Philippines went well enough for the U.S., the Japanese Army on Luzon, swelled to 65,000 men by early December, resisted fiercely. The U.S. Sixth Army came up against well-fortified positions, including tunnels and caves, the enemy even resorting to some isolated trench warfare. However, by constantly reinforcing the landing points and bringing in fresh units, the U.S. forces, who enjoyed air superiority over the battle areas, made steady progress. With the newly arrived 77th Infantry Division, the Americans fought their way to capture the main objectives. MacArthur made his well publicised return to the islands on January 9, wading ashore on Luzon from an LST.

Half of Yamashita's defense force on Luzon was composed of the "Kembu" Group, a 30,000-strong army under Maj-Gen. Rikichi Tsukada, billeted around the central plain and the surrounding mountains, primarily to guard Clark Field. Griswold's unit first encountered Tsukada's troops on January 23, and heavy fighting ensued. By the end of the month Clark Field had been recaptured by XIV Corps at a cost of more than enemy 2,500 dead. The rest had scattered into the hills. Griswold was then able to resume his march on Manila where wresting the Filipino capital from the enemy led to the only house-to-house fighting of the Pacific war. In the meantime, XI Corps (Maj-Gen. Charles P. Hall) and the 328th Infantry Division, with a regiment of the 24th Division, had landed on the west coast of Luzon with the intention of driving to the north of the Bataan Peninsula to secure Manila Bay and the Olongapo naval base.

Yamashita avoided a repeat of MacArthur's withdrawal and entrapment on Bataan in 1942, and instead fought it out with Hall's forces, who

consequently took two weeks to reach Manila Bay. A second landing took place on February 3, when paratroops of the 11th Airborne Division dropped south of the bay to tie down the enemy until the rest of the division dropped at a point inland. When the 11th joined up, it moved on Manila planning to secure it quickly.

This plan only partially succeeded as stubborn enemy resistance halted the U.S. advance. It was clear that the only way to secure Manila rapidly was from the north. MacArthur gave emphatic confirmation that the troops should, "Go to Manila," in any way possible. The task fell to Griswold's 37th Infantry and the tanks of the recently arrived 1st Cavalry Division.

An early worry for the Americans was removed when the Santo Thomas internment camp was liberated by a flying column of 1st Cavalry's tanks. Northern Manila was in American hands, but the rest of the city held some 17,000 enemy troops, naval personnel under the command of Rear-Adm. Sanji Iwabachi. Like MacArthur before him, Yamashita had no wish to see the Philippine capital destroyed—but his naval comrade had no such qualms. Iwabachi saw it as his duty to delay the Americans as long as possible, thereby postponing the invasion of Japan. He sent separate battle groups to fight for every street and proceeded to put the city to the torch. These fires ignit-

Above: Espiritu Santo in the New Hebrides became one of the major supply points for the central Pacific campaign as the war moved nearer to Japan. Here, the carrier USS *Saratoga* and cruiser USS *Montpelier* guard oilers and freighters.

Above Right: The U.S. Marines became adept at amphibious operations, although not all landings were unopposed as this on Guadalcanal.

Right: Airfields were the key to victory in the Pacific, those in the New Hebrides being early acquisitions vital to the U.S. Espiritu Santo had a single strip with dispersed aircraft revetments.

ed others, especially in poor districts where shanties burned like tinder. The Japanese concurrently embarked on an orgy of atrocities against civilians. During the heavy fighting to clear each section of the city, the Americans had little choice but to use considerable firepower to winkle out the tenacious Japanese. Artillery fire inevitably caused widespread destruction and an enormous number of civilian casualties, MacArthur having foresworn the extensive use of airpower on the grounds that it would cause heavy civilian casualties! Observers believed artillery fire to be worse in this respect. Condemned to hand-to-hand fighting, U.S. troops used any weapon to kill the crazed Japanese, including flame-throwers.

When Manila was finally in American hands —by early March—the fighting was far from

-1-1897) (10-12-43-1500) (12" 3500) BOMBER 2 ESPIRITU SANTO

Left and Below Left: Under siege, the Japanese tried desperately to camouflage precious shipping from prying U.S. reconnaissance. West of Lingayen, at Santiago Island and Cape Solinao on January 9, 1945, the cameras still picked out several small boat targets.

Below: The British Eastern Fleet returned to Ceylon in 1945 to use the excellent and largely undamaged facilities of Colombo harbor. An armoured carrier, either *Formidable* or *Illustrious*, and the battleship *Warspite* dominate this tranquil scene.

over; MacArthur, determined to oversee the liberation of the entire Philippine archipelago, ordered his troops to engage the enemy in numerous small but costly battles. Airpower often prevented these actions from becoming prolonged, but Yamashita, who refused to surrender and survived the war to be hanged for war crimes, was still in combat when news of Japan's surrender was received. By then the protracted battle to secure the Philippines had cost the United States' forces some 47,000 casualties.

INTO THE MEAT GRINDER

6. TAKING IWO JIMA

BACKGROUND

The continuing need to secure air bases as near to Japan as possible boosted the central Pacific offensive, spearheaded by the U.S. Navy, Marines, and Army with substantial Allied support. With air bases in the Marianas well able to handle multiple wings of B-29s, a glance at a map of the world's largest ocean nevertheless shows how far the Superfortress crews had to fly to bomb Japan—even from the Marianas the round trip was 3,000 miles. What was needed was a half-way point able to accommodate crippled bombers flying back from the home islands, and to serve as a base for long-range escort fighters. Iwo Jima, the porkchop-shaped volcanic chunk in the Bonins group, was the only realistic choice.

B-24 Liberators of the Seventh Air Force had begun bombing Iwo Jima as early as August 1944, and raids had been gradually stepped up to the point where bombers were over the island virtually around the clock. Two B-29 strikes were made before the U.S. landings took place on February 17, 1945, by which time about 6,800 tons of bombs and 22,000 shells had been directed at the Japanese fortifications. This deluge of fire was mostly designed to prevent reinforcements reaching Iwo's defenders, although these still got through.

Unknown to U.S. commanders, Iwo Jima's defenses were more substantial than anything they had previously come across. The Japanese had had ample time to dig gun positions into every suitable piece of earth, and to tunnel out a veritable honeycomb of caves which housed personnel shelters, artillery positions, and machine

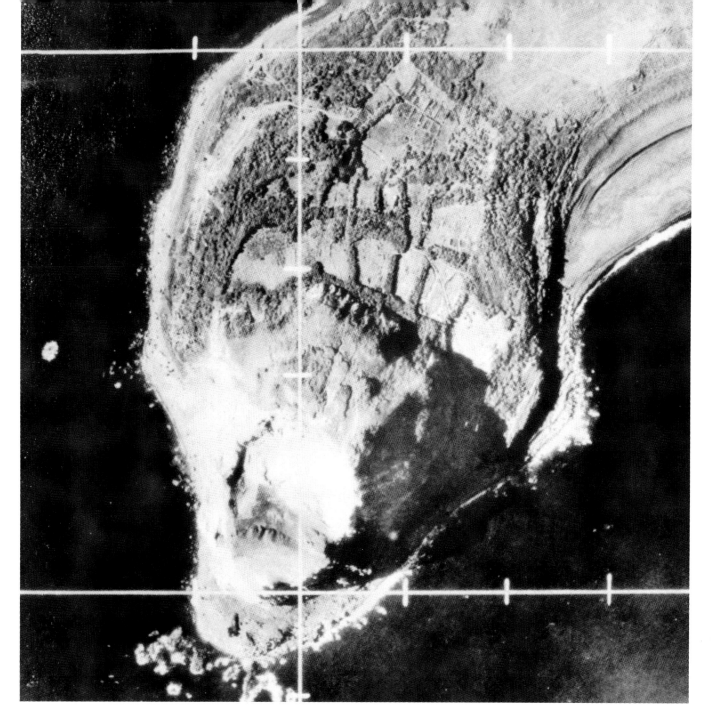

Above: An aerial view of Iwo Jima taken on Dog-Day plus five, showing Mt. Suribachi and transports anchored in the bay beyond.

Left: Shipboard photos of the bombardment of Iwo Jima on December 8, 1944, showing shells exploding over six miles distant.

gun nests. Mortars were located anywhere that the simple firing tripod would stand up. These could be fired off and whipped back under cover so that very few mortars—or any other weapons—were visible to reconnaissance flights. Lt-Gen. Tadamichi Kuribayashi, who had been made responsible for turning Iwo Jima into a fortress with 600 pillboxes and gun emplacements, had done his work with incredible efficiency. The Vth Amphibious Corps, comprising the 3rd, 4th, and 5th Marine Divisions, was about to find out how well.

THE BATTLE

Covered for the most part in brown, volcanic ash from Mount Suribachi, an inactive volcano rising 550ft about sea level, Iwo Jima is 4.5 miles long by 2.5 miles wide. Beaches covered in ash extend along the northern and eastern shorelines, which in 1945 made reasonable landing points for an invasion fleet. By the time the Americans were ready to land, there were two airfields with a third under construction.

Admiral Kelly Turner ordered the force to go at 06.45 on February 19. In almost perfect weather the attack unfolded. It was soon in trouble. As the first waves hit the beaches, the volcanic ash quickly bogged down the amphtracs

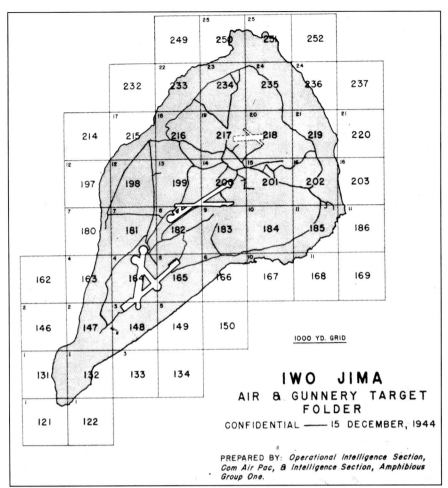

IWO JIMA

AIR & GUNNERY TARGET
FOLDER

CONFIDENTIAL —— 15 DECEMBER, 1944

PREPARED BY: *Operational Intelligence Section,
Com Air Pac, & Intelligence Section, Amphibious
Group One.*

1000 YD. GRID

Left: A map prepared for the Iwo Jima air and gunnery target folder dated December 15, 1944, and showing the island divided into a grid of 1,000-yard squares.

Right: Photographic close-ups enabled the terrain in each grid square to be studied closely. This is target square 199 and part of 200 that include the runway of what was initially known as airfield No. 1 and later as South Field.

Below Right: Part of target square 164 and 165 showing Iwo Jima's other airfield.

and the Marines, swept by murderous fire, had no natural cover. Their one chance was the friendly warships which proceeded to lay fire along the shoreline, dropping shells in rolling barrages as close as 200 yards from the crouching men. The result was that the commanding enemy positions on Mt. Suribachi could not be brought to bear on the left flank of the 5th Marine Division. The battleships *Santa Fe* and *Nevada* were the stars of the show, their gunnery being particularly effective.

With nightfall of D (Dog)-Day, 30,000 troops were ashore—and the Marines had taken 2,420 casualties with 519 killed. Darkness did not bring the expected suicidal charge as Kuribayashi, knowing that he had little hope of reinforcement, opted to conserve his forces and fight for every yard of soil. This meant that to get inland the Marines had to work their way yard by yard across exposed ground, a terrible ordeal for the participants.

To assist the troops, the Navy allocated direct gunfire support by destroyers to every Marine battalion; at daybreak, the ships poured fire into their designated sector of beach. As the troops moved forward, the ships waited to provide deep fire support as confirmed by spotter planes

or shore fire-control parties. The air groups aboard jeep carriers meanwhile flew CAP and close support sorties from dawn until dusk. Some kamikaze activity materialized, the carriers *Saratoga* and *Bismarck Sea* being hit and the latter sunk; otherwise, this form of enemy reaction was all but absent off Iwo Jima.

Through the end of January and into February the struggle for control of the island went on. Then, on February 23, Colonel Harry "the Horse" Liversedge sent 40 men of the 3rd Marines to scale Suribachi. A small flag was duly planted after a firefight with the remaining Japanese, before a larger, more visible flag was brought up. When this flag was finally raised, the troops were heartened, despite the fact that the battle was only partially over.

Steady, bunker by bunker, cave by cave progress had, by February 25, pushed the Japanese back to an enclave in the northern part of the island. To finish it General Schmidt of the 3rd Marine Division positioned three regiments to advance in line abreast. This succeeded, although all organized Japanese resistance did not end until March 16. The cost was 6,891 Marines killed and 18,070 wounded. The Japanese had sacrificed 20,703 men in an ultimately futile defense with only 316 being taken prisoner in this main phase of combat. Another 867 were captured during April and May as isolated pockets continued to hold out.

Seabees were on the island soon after the first waves of Marines had landed, and in the face of sniper fire had surveyed the most suitable areas for extending the existing Japanese airstrips. On

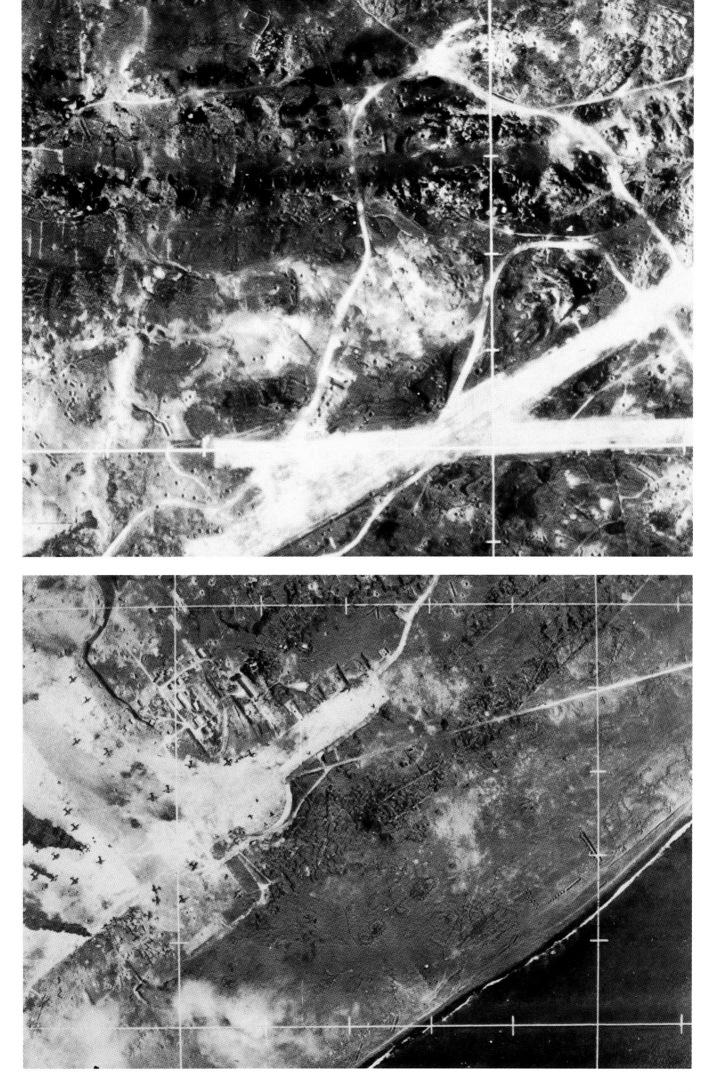

Left: A view from the Sky Control position of the cruiser *Salt Lake City* as she fires her aft main gun battery at Iwo Jima on December 8, 1944.

Below left: An OS2U Kingfisher scout floatplane, with wingtip damage from enemy fire, after return to the parent ship. Floatplanes performed valuable service in spotting for the guns during offshore bombardments.

Right: Occasionally Japanese return fire found the range. An unidentified U.S. warship exhibits superficial damage.

Below: One difficulty in island bombardment was that shells occasionally went right over the target to hazard ships off the opposite shore. During the Iwo Jima operation one shell, probably fired by units off the Western side of the island, narrowly missed the cruiser *Vicksburg.*

March 4 the hard work of the construction troops paid off when the first B-29 landed. Not without sustaining their own casualties, the Seabees were vital to the final outcome of the island occupation. By the war's end a total of 2,400 B-29s had sought a haven on Iwo Jima. The busiest period was the night of June 8/9 when 93 aircraft put down with varying degrees of damage—that at least was a partial repayment for the American lives that had been lost in taking the place. Hundreds of crews knew that without Iwo's welcoming runways they might never have survived.

It had been the intention to escort the B-29s to Japan as soon as a base could be made available to the best long-range fighter in the AAF inventory, the P-51 Mustang. With Iwo Jima declared free of enemy troops, the Seventh AAF in Hawaii dispatched the 15th Fighter Group to the Volcano Islands. The Mustang pilots, many of whom had been sitting on their hands for months, welcomed the chance of some action. It was not long in coming. Following a number of ground attack sorties, the first long-range escort mission was laid on for April 7.

Other Mustang groups moved to Iwo, the varying strength of enemy opposition to Superfortress raids being such that Seventh AAF could subsequently afford to dispatch fighter missions primarily to strafe targets in Japan, particularly airfields. By indirectly taking the heat off the bombers in this way, the Pacific P-51 force was probably as effective as it was on escort duties—not that the latter stopped, and with P-61 night fighters based on Iwo Jima and, shortly afterward, squadrons of very long-range P-47N Thunderbolts stationed on Ie Shima, the Seventh and Fifth Air Forces shared in much of the "eleventh hour" air action in the Central Pacific.

The late 1944/early 1945 period was marked by an enormous Army Air effort in parallel with those of land-based Marine and Navy units. General George Kenney's Fifth Air Force completed the long road back from the jungle strips of New Guinea to bring its predominantly medium bomber and fighter-equipped force forward to fly from various recaptured island bases from the Philippines to the Ryukus. One squadron of Kenney's 312th Bomb Group converted to the B-32 Dominator, the four-engined insurance policy against B-29 failure, for a few last cracks at the exhausted Japanese.

While the Seventh's fighters took front-line billing, its bomber force, always modest in size, continued to fly B-24s to pound stubborn enemy pockets of resistance miles behind what had become in effect three different ocean fronts. Numerous Japanese pockets remained and it was important that these be contained and unable to hamper Allied operations, even in rear areas.

SUBMARINES SUPREME

Increasingly giving up its conquered territories to the Allies on land, the IJN was all but powerless to prevent the Japanese mercantile marine being remorselessly whittled down by surface forces, air attacks, and, particularly, by American submarines. The fleet submarine force became one of the most successful in the history of undersea warfare as it pursued a dedicated campaign of destruction across the Pacific.

Unlike the Allies in the Atlantic, the Japanese paid little heed to the merit of mutual protection of merchant ships under a convoy system, and continued to dispatch small numbers of ships—often even singly—into dangerous, enemy-dominated waters. The results were predictable; thousands of tons of supplies never reached their would-be recipients and thousands of troops perished before ever setting foot on the land areas they were sent to reinforce. The Japanese failed, despite such setbacks, to change their tactics, and their ships continued to fall victim to marauding submarines. The toll spiraled to incredible heights in the last two years of the war as ship after ship plunged to a watery grave. Ships also fell foul of U.S. aerial- and sea-laid mines to the point where no part of the ocean was really safe for unarmed and largely unprotected freighters.

With her assets whittled almost to the point of impotency, the IJN could no longer provide adequate escort to transports, although she had never done so to the same degree as the Allies.

Above Right: A view of one of the landing beaches on Iwo Jima taken at 08.15, H-45 on D-Day.

Center Right: Aerial observer's view of the fleet bombarding Iwo Jima.

Right: Ground support air strike on Iwo Jima on February 20, 1945, looking north from 3,500ft and showing bomb bursts in the center of the island.

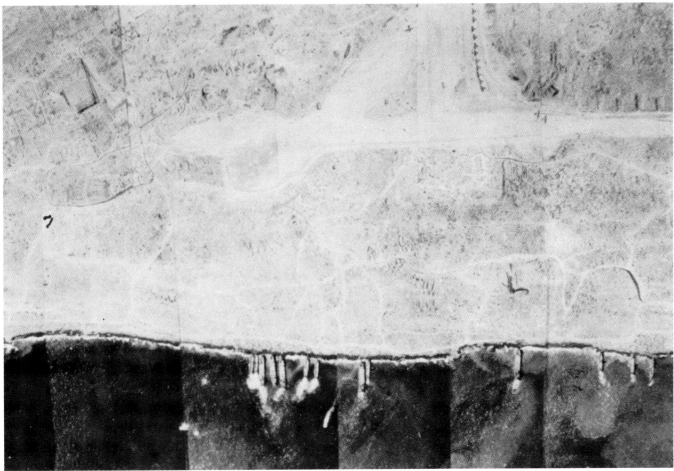

Left: An April 11, 1945, photo showing the field of fire from a Japanese five-inch gun battery located in a cliff overlooking the eastern beaches of Iwo Jima.

Above Left: The same five-inch gun emplacement after being knocked out by U.S. fire.

Top: The flamethrower was the best weapon to flush out defenders hidden in tunnels and pillboxes.

Above: Mosiac vertical of Iwo's East and West beaches on D-Day+16, March 7, 1945.

OPERATION "ICEBERG"

7. THE BATTLE FOR OKINAWA

BACKGROUND

As an American ring of steel closed inexorably around Japan, preparations were made to secure the last major hurdle to launching air strikes within comfortable range. Okinawa, largest of the Ryukyu Island group lying some 350 miles southwest of Honshu, represented the final bastion in the Japanese outer defensive perimeter. Once Okinawa had been taken, the way to Japan was wide open, the island being ideally placed to serve as a staging area when the seaborne invasion of Japan inevitably came around. For all these reasons, mastery of Okinawa would be bitterly contested.

Surrounded by coral reefs, during the last year of the war Okinawa supported a population of some 435,000 people in numerous peasant farming communities, the inhabitants of which were regarded as inferior by the Japanese. Although the islands had been annexed by Japan in 1879, little had since been done to improve their low standard of living, although Okinawan youths were drafted into the Japanese military.

During the war—from September 1944 when the Marianas fell—Okinawa was garrisoned and fortified, the Japanese thinking nothing of commandeering native burial tombs which dotted the entire island, to turn them into local points of defense. As far as more major defensive positions were concerned, the limestone hills made them ideal for the kind of tunneling at which Japanese engineers excelled.

From a military viewpoint, the most important area of Okinawa was the low coastal plain running from Zamba Point on which the island's two main airfields, Yontan and Kadena, were situated. In addition, there were three other airfields and two bays on the eastern side which were useful anchorages. Off the northern tip of Okinawa lay the small, virtually flat island of Ie Shima. In the spring of 1945 it was to prove that modest size did not represent easy conquest.

Attractive though Okinawa was as a U.S. base—it was actually part of one of Japan's pre-

Below: U.S. amphibious forces hit the beach at Aware, Tokishiki Shima in the Ryukyu Islands.

Top: U.S. Marines crossing a bridge built by engineers over the Asotokawa River on Okinawa.

Above: Invasion craft at Hagushi beaches, Okinawa on L-Day.

Left: A section of Itoman town on Okinawa with a U.S. tank moving up one of the streets.

Below Left: Overflight photo of a village settlement on Okinawa, which had a larger civilian population than any other island of comparable size stormed by U.S. troops.

fectures and close enough to allow medium bombers to attack the home islands—it was a considerable distance from the nearest American supply point. Ammunition, fuel, and most other items, particularly the construction materials and personnel needed to sustain the island as a base, would have to be brought in by sea. Though not considered a major problem, the presence of Okinawa's civilian population had to be allowed for in the military equation.

Squeezing Japan into her last remaining island territory was also a factor, in that there was little doubt that the Japanese would concentrate all remaining air and seapower in trying to repel the U.S. invasion. There were about 120 airfields available to the Japanese air forces within striking distance of Okinawa, this figure including around 65 on Formosa, 360 miles away. The rest were on Kyushu and the Chinese mainland.

In the period between landing troops and the securing Okinawa's airfields, the defense of the amphibious force would be entirely in the hands of the Navy. This fact naturally worried Nimitz, although as one of the joint commanders of the Twentieth Air Force, he had the authority to call on the B-29 force in the Marianas to indirectly support the Okinawa assault by bombing airfields in Japan. This he did on several occasions, otherwise the Navy's carrier air groups would have to cope with the veritable deluge of fire anticipated from the Japanese. This started some weeks before a man had set a foot on an Okinawan beach.

Having refueled his carriers on March 16, Spruance made a fast run in towards Japan and launched air strikes on Kyushu on the 17th. On the 18th the enemy reacted and damaged two carriers in kamikaze attacks, but a critical Japanese attack came on the 19th when a single kamikaze aircraft hit the USS *Franklin*. As rockets, bombs and aircraft began to detonate, the carrier was swept by fire and was all but

Below: Naha town, Okinawa, showing the deadly work of aircraft of Task Force 58 on the harbor installations and shipping.

Left: The interior of Okinawa was subject to massive bombardment by carrier task forces for the duration of Japanese resistance.

Right: A division of TBF Avengers from the light carrier USS *Bataan* overflies the east coast of Okinawa.

Below Right: View of Okinawa, taken by USS *Essex* aircraft on March 1, 1945, looking southeast, reveals Naha airfield with the town and harbor to the left.

abandoned by her surviving crew, with 724 men killed or posted missing in the inferno.

Listing badly and well ablaze, the *Franklin* seemed to be doomed, but with outstanding seamanship on the part of Captain Leslie Gehres and a skeleton crew, the *Franklin* was brought back onto an even keel, taken in tow, and finally was able to make her way out of the battle area under her own steam, to complete a 12,000-mile voyage to New York.

The Japanese had also struck a blow, albeit indirectly, against the *Enterprise*. It was "friendly" AAA fire that started fires aboard and rendering her deck temporarily unusable for sorties by her night air group. *Yorktown* had also been crippled by a bomb hit on March 18.

These temporary setbacks did not hold up the invasion. Some of the outlying Ryukyu Islands were taken before Okinawa was tackled, and by March 26 all these objectives were under U.S.

control. Kerama Retto was secured on the 27th, and acted as a useful base during Operation "Iceberg," but Tokashi Jima, the second largest island, was not invaded, leaving about 300 enemy troops in the hills until the end of the war.

"ICEBERG" BEGINS

Reconnaissance of Okinawa failed to show a living soul visible to the aerial cameras. The Americans were mystified to understand how so many enemy troops and civilians could simply disappear. Strangest of all was the fact that no fire greeted the overflights. Not for a moment did commanders expect the landings to be unopposed, despite assurances from prisoners that Okinawa had been evacuated

"Iceberg" began on April 1, 1945—L (Love)-Day to the men involved.

In command of the amphibious forces was Vice-Adm. Turner, with nearly 1,000 aircraft positioned to protect the landing ships. These, part of a fleet totalling 1,457 vessels, would convey the new U.S. Tenth Army under Lt-Gen. Simon Bolivar Buckner to the designated beaches.

Buckner's command represented 154,000 combat troops, comprising XXIV Corps (Maj-Gen. Hodge, U.S. Army) and II Amphibious Corps (Maj-Gen. Geiger, USMC), each with two divisions, plus the 2nd Marine Division, 77th Infantry Division, and 27th Infantry Division. Other units swelled Buckner's command to 183,000 men, and even this figure would be increased by the time the operation was completed to total more than half a million men.

Few participants had any illusion that this would not be the big one; with the tenacious enemy defense of Iwo Jima still fresh in the memory, the first men who splashed ashore on Okinawa that Easter Sunday hardly expected to get off the beaches alive. They were wrong.

Before the battle U.S. intelligence had noted that Okinawa had seen a gradual build-up of troops, and immediately prior to "Iceberg" the garrison had swelled to between 53,000 and 56,000 Japanese including infantry, artillery, service, and naval troops. The figure also encompassed the personnel of a single tank regiment. In terms of enemy hardware, the Americans faced an array of artillery, mortars, and machine guns. The armored regiment was estimated to have about 95 examples of light and medium tanks.

After pouring a huge barrage of shells onto Okinawa, the beaches of Hagushi were stormed by waves of LSTs, LSMs, landing craft, and boats, each one color-coded to ensure they grounded on the designated beach. Beach markers were set by the first wave ashore as a guide to those following.

As the first troops hit the beaches, it seemed for a time that the reports of enemy evacuation were indeed true. The shoreline was all but empty. In fact Japanese commander Lt-Gen. Mitsuru Ushijima's strategy was not to oppose the landings but to let the Americans make their way inland.

With some 50,000 troops getting ashore unloading proceeded, still unhampered by

Above: American battleships standing 2,000-3,000 yards off-shore to cover the landings on Okinawa on L-Day, April 1, 1945.

Right: Aerial camera view from aircraft of *Yorktown* (CV-10) as the first wave of landing craft heads for the Okinawan beaches on April 1, 1945. Smoke drifts from a salvo of rockets fired into the beach by support craft.

Above: Yontan Airfield on Okinawa under attack on October 10, 1944.

enemy fire, this situation prevailing until nightfall on L-Day, the precious hours of peaceful daylight being highly appreciated by all concerned. By 10.35 in the morning of L+1, the troops walked onto the edge of one of Okinawa's prime targets, Kadena airfield. By midday, Yontan was also secured, no less than three days earlier than the airfields had been scheduled for capture.

Throughout L-Day no Japanese aircraft had appeared and no fire swept the northern beaches. In the south, only a few rounds of light artillery fire and the occasional mortar round disturbed the uneasy air of calm. Still no enemy troop movements were revealed to air reconnaissance.

At 14.00 Admiral Turner ordered unloading to continue through the night; artillery and tons of vital supplies poured ashore as troops continued to fan out across the island. Vehicles of all kinds—including amphtracs, tanks, DUKWs, LSTs carrying bridges and causeway sets, and ammunition carriers—all made their way inshore to park in their allotted spaces, as the troops penetrated further inland—and began to outrun their supplies. Meanwhile Ushijima stuck to his orders and waited. He had in fact over 100,000 troops burrowed into the fortifications of Okinawa.

Offshore, some kamikaze activity and bombing—and vivid imaginations—started some small scale fire fights to little purpose. Several of the transports, pulled off the landing areas for safety, were hit.

Dawn on L+1 found the sailors still searching for invisible Japanese ashore, although there were plenty airborne around the fleet. CAPs shot down the majority of those which posed a threat, although some inevitably reached the transports and their escorts. At Kerama Retto the Marines had men wounded and equipment lost to a kamikaze that struck an LST.

Making its way inland, on April 4 XXIV Corps finally approached the point where most of the Japanese garrison was entrenched. This was in the southern part of the island along the Kakazu Ridge, the enemy having also fortified two other defensive lines—the Machinato and Shuri lines. Combat was joined, and the battle raged for eight days. On May 4, Ushijima counter-attacked, failed to achieve any advantage, and lost 5,000 men in the process.

Buckner pressed forward, making slow progress against the in-depth enemy defense. Sugar Loaf and Conical Hills were the scene of intense fighting, the latter not being secured until the second half of May when the 96th

Division finally ejected the enemy. The survivors withdrew to make a stand at Yaeju Dake Escarpment, and it took Buckner until June 14 to break through this position—but when they did so the Marines made short work of the defenders and within days the area was the scene of little more than mopping-up operations. This is not to minimize the achievement of reaching that point; the ferocity of the fighting for Okinawa stunned the world and indirectly led to the decision by the United States to seek any alternative means to an invasion of Japan.

On April 16, Ie Shima was invaded. Required primarily to base a vital radar, the island was subsequently used as a forward fighter strip for some of the last Army Air Force sorties to Japan. The 77th Division fought for it until the 21st, when among the resulting casualties was the popular war correspondent Ernie Pyle, killed by machine gun fire as he was following front line troops.

Above: Smoke and fires observed from offshore as the air strike on Yontan airfield unfolds on October 10, 1944.

Right: One of many camouflaged pillboxes that defended Okinawa, this was a mutual support point for a larger, concrete blockhouse and an elaborate system of machine gun positions and trenches. All were abandoned by the enemy on L-Day.

Right: A Japanese vessel under attack and exploding on March 28, 1945.

KAMIKAZES

Kamikaze sorties reached a crescendo during the Okinawa operation, and radar picket destroyers were one of the principal measures deployed to provide early warning of their approach. The problem was that, until the airfields ashore could accept U.S. aircraft, the carrier-based air cover finished at dusk as the escort carriers could not launch in darkness and the few night fighters available to TF-58 could not be spared to guard the pickets. Darkness did not stop the kamikaze attacks, one of the worst taking place on May 3/4, when 370 officers and men, two destroyers, and two LSMs were lost.

The sixth big attack—out of a total of ten made on TF-58—was on May 10/11 and was even worse. This was the occasion that the *Bunker Hill* was struck with the loss of nearly 400 men. Further personnel casualties were caused when the picket station destroyer screen was hit hard.

The kamikaze ethos, fostered by the IJN in the first place, was brought to a terrible climax in April 1945. In a final, desperate and typically futile gesture of defiance, the IJN made an attempt to disrupt U.S. operations at Okinawa by sacrificing the battleship *Yamato.* Carrying only enough fuel for a one-way voyage, this was a suicide mission pure and simple. The Japanese task force, otherwise comprising the cruiser

Yahagi and eight destroyers, was commanded by Vice-Adm. Seiichi Ito. Mitscher, taking no chances, sent three task groups with about 380 aircraft to intercept the IJN ships long before they could close with his transports unloading off Okinawa. Ito's considerable complement of AAA guns failed to repel continual attacks by U.S. Navy carrier aircraft and the 71,000-ton *Yamato,* the last of two examples of the largest battleships ever built, went down on April 7 smothered by bomb and torpedo hits. Four Japanese destroyers shared her watery grave.

The outcome of the battle for Okinawa was never in doubt, nor was the ability of American forces to overcome any obstacle the Japanese might put in their way—that much augured well for the invasion of the home islands. The "X factor" was the cost: Okinawa had shown that unless some other way of persuading the enemy to end the war could be found, an invasion of the home islands would bring horrendous casualties.

The ritual suicide of General Ushijima and his Chief of Staff, General Cho, marked the end of the Okinawan campaign and the career of the Japanese Thirty-second Army. In 83 days of bitter fighting to the final securing of Hill 85 on June 22, the U.S. Tenth Army had achieved victory, but at terrible cost—the largest in any campaign in the Pacific war. Among the men killed was Lt-Gen. Buckner, victim of a bullet ricochet from a nearby rock as he stood watching one of the final skirmishes on June 18. Total American battle casualties amounted to 49,151, of which 15,520 were killed. At sea the Navy had 36 ships sunk (many to kamikaze attack) and 368 damaged while aircraft losses totaled 763.

BRITISH PACIFIC FLEET (BPF)

"Iceberg" also saw the involvement of the British Pacific Fleet, alias Task Force 57. On November 22, this fleet came under the operational command of Vice-Adm. Sir Bernard Rawlings, second in command to Admiral Sir Bruce Fraser, who took considerable pride in his small force being given such status. With the fleet carriers *Indomitable, Illustrious, Indefatigable,* and *Victorious* capable of launching a total of 244 aircraft, TF-57 also comprised two battleships, cruisers, destroyers, and for the first time in the RN, a fleet replenishment train.

The British contingent guarded the flank of the main "Iceberg" operation by pounding the Sakishima Islands lying 150 southwest of Okinawa. A sizable force of kamikazes was based in these islands and, as expected, the RN ships became "Divine Wind" targets. However, the British carriers were tough nuts to crack. The suicide pilots were either ignorant of, or unable to distinguish, the fact that the British carriers had armored, steel flightdecks, unlike their U.S. Navy counterparts with wooden deck planking. While kamikazes did not exactly bounce off when they hit the British carriers, heavy blows which would have curtailed operations from U.S. ships for a considerable time, did not impede the RN carriers for longer than a few hours.

A series of raids on the Sumatran oil refineries at Pangkalan (December 20, 1944) and Palembang on January 24 and 29, 1945, denied the Japanese a vital source of fuel at a very critical time. The latter raids, which totally destroyed the refineries, were the largest carrier-borne operations ever mounted by the Royal Navy during the war.

Concurrent with the formation of the BPF, the smaller East Indies Fleet was created for operations in the Indian Ocean. Built initially around five escort carriers (more would be added later) this latter naval force found little "trade" as the Japanese focussed increasingly on home defense.

In direct support for "Iceberg," the BPF's air groups continued their attacks on Japanese airfields during April and May, the months when all the fleet carriers, on station on a rotational basis, were hit by kamikazes. Although no ships were fatally damaged, they went back to their home base in Sydney for any repairs, operational commitments permitting. For the British carriers it was not so much damage to the ships the kamikazes caused but the loss of aircraft (despite fleet replenishment) that forced them out of the line to pick up replacements.

On August 9 the BPF sent a flight of 1841 Squadron Corsair fighter-bombers from *Formidable* to attack some of the remaining Japanese warships anchored in Onagawa Wan Bay. The ships put up a deadly wall of AAA fire as the single-seaters plunged down. One of the Corsair pilots, Canadian Lt. Robert Gray RCNVR, planted a bomb squarely on a destroyer, which went down. But Gray was killed when his aircraft failed to pull out of its dive. He was awarded a posthumous Victoria Cross, the only one earned by a Fleet Air Arm pilot flying from a carrier deck during the war. It was a fitting, if sad, end to an outstanding period of operations by the capital ships of the Royal Navy of which *Indefatigable* had the honor of being the last BPF carrier on station with the American fleet on VJ-Day.

Right: The superbattleship *Yamato* was expended on a futile, one-way suicide mission on April 7, 1945. Caught by aircraft of TF-58 she was photographed hit and burning.

THE "DIVINE WIND"

8. KAMIKAZE AND THE MANHATTAN PROJECT

BACKGROUND

American sailors only gradually became aware of what came to be known as the "kamikazes" during the invasion of the Philippines—although as early as the Pearl Harbor operation, midget submarines had embarked upon sorties in which the crews were not expected to return. Other incidents of sea and airborne suicide sorties followed, but it was shortly before the invasion of Luzon on October 15, 1944, that Soemu Toyoda, C-in-C of the Combined Fleet, gave his blessing to the establishment of an aerial suicide corps

In a number of earlier seemingly unrelated incidents, Japanese airmen were observed not to bail out of their stricken aircraft but stay with them to their inevitable doom. One such incident actually took place on October 15, the day the kamikaze corps was officially sanctioned. That day Masafumi Arima, CO of the 26th Air Flotilla, deliberately crashed his aircraft on the carrier USS *Franklin*. In the understandable confusion, this strike was reported as two hits by conventional bombs—the result for the American carrier sailors was much the same.

Whether or not this and other crashes were deliberate was hard to prove in the heat of battle, and proved a vexing question for the U.S. Navy. There could be numerous reasons for these apparent suicidal crashes, and few then realized that the kamikaze, the "Divine Wind," was soon to be part of a deliberate policy.

By recruiting a volunteer force of young, idealistic pilots willing to sacrifice themselves for the glory of Japan, the war leaders indulged in desperate measures indeed. In her death throes, the nation sought a counter to overwhelming Allied might; the kamikazes seemed to be the answer: if every downed aircraft could take an enemy ship with it, the American fleets would be decimated and ultimately routed, or so the

Below: Photo of a recognition model released to U.S. forces showing the release of a Yokosuka MXY7 Baka bomb from a Mitsubishi G4M "Betty" bomber acting as a "mother ship."

Above: Many abandoned Bakas were found by U.S. troops after the Japanese surrender, that in the foreground bearing dotted markings for measuring dimensions.

optimistic Japanese warlords believed. Those who viewed the survival of Japan as demanding a "fight to the death" bloodbath still held much sway, and the kamikazes were one result of this attitude. Indeed, the call for suicide pilots was enthusiastically answered, although by no means all Japanese airmen believed in this barbaric method of warfare.

As a tactical expedient, the idea had a macabre economy, considering Japan's position. Pilot training was cut to the minimum. Men were required to perform one take off, and the aircraft used needed only to be flyable and able to carry at least one bomb. Almost anything able to stagger into the air could be used for a kamikaze sortie. So went the theory.

The first Special Attack units were formed using conventional Army and Navy aircraft—fighters were preferred due to their speed—with personnel drawn from regular units. That soon changed to a policy of raising new units solely for the purpose of carrying out suicide attacks.

There were also moves to streamline the concept. The risks in using conventional aircraft against high performance U.S. Navy interceptors, that, on equal terms, had the edge on anything the Japanese could put into the air, were all too clear. If the kamikazes were wiped out before they came anywhere near their targets—something the defenders obviously tried to achieve on every occasion they appeared—then the entire process was a complete waste of lives. All they would bring Japan was a little more time.

BAKA, THE "HUMAN BOMB"

In 1944 contracts were agreed for the manufacture of a more sophisticated weapon, one built specifically for the kamikaze mission. The first result was the Yokosuka XY7 Baka, a tiny aircraft powered by a cluster of rocket motors and consisting of a rudimentary cockpit, fuel storage, and a warhead. Carried to its target area by a Mitsubishi B4N "Betty" mother ship the Baka was strictly a "one way" weapon. Ostensibly the most effective method of bringing the effect of the "Divine Wind" down on the enemy, as it was too fast to be intercepted and too small for ship-borne guns to track, the Baka largely failed.

On March 21, 1945, the day of the first official launch, nothing was achieved. Baka's weak point was the delivery method; the "Betty" was relatively slow and easy meat for the prowling Hellcats and Corsairs that protected the U.S. fleet. Nicknamed the "Flying Lighter," the Mitsubishi bomber's propensity to burn was legendary, and most Baka carriers (few of which saw combat) were shot down before they could release their warload and its hapless pilot.

The first Baka attack recognized as such by the Americans on the receiving end, took place

on April 12 when the bombs sank the destroyer *Mannert L. Abele*. The news of this startling development was overshadowed by the death of Roosevelt.

Later models of the Baka were to have had turbojet power, but again the vulnerability of the parent aircraft remained the Achilles' heel. There was no time left to test, much less bring into service, a mother ship with the performance needed to successfully evade U.S. Navy interceptors.

Conventional kamikaze aircraft fared little better in terms of sinking the capital ships that were their prime targets, and hundreds were destroyed before they could crash the decks of American ships.

A system of picket ships—destroyers patrolling a few miles offshore—were positioned specifically to detect incoming enemy aircraft on radar. Radio links to shore bases and carriers alerted the duty combat air patrol which would immediately scramble fighters to intercept.

The Japanese soon recognized the threat posed by the destroyer pickets and made every effort to sink them. Accounts of destroyer crews surviving incredible damage from numerous kamikaze strikes went round the fleet to garner deserved respect and deep admiration. Many sailors, kept at "general quarters" with their

Left: On April 11, 1945, a "Zeke" kamikaze came in at main deck level to break up on the starboard side of the battleship *Missouri*. The aircraft only scratched some paint off the "Mighty Mo'."

Below: View from the stern of a cruiser (possibly *Pittsburgh* or *Santa Fe*) during efforts to take the carrier *Franklin*, hit by bombs on March 19, 1944, in tow. *Franklin* eventually got home under her own power.

ships "buttoned up" for days on end, died or suffered terrible wounds in the ships that were hit. Kamikazes sank a number of ships and managed a total of 2,940 sorties flown between October 1944 and August 1945, a huge effort that failed in its primary purpose. That the Japanese were obviously holding back aircraft for the Allied invasion was reflected in the fact that just seven machines flew on the last recorded kamikaze attack, on August 15.

Employing an utterly terrifying form of warfare, the kamikaze pilots were feared and respected by U.S. sailors who bore the brunt of their attempt to die gloriously—as they saw it. Probably the worst aspect of the kamikaze ethos was that it indirectly signed the death warrants of thousands of the very people it was meant to save.

In planning for Operation "Olympic," the amphibious invasion of the home islands, Allied estimates of the likely opposition had to assume that friendly forces would be subjected to mass attacks by suicide planes and boats. This is exactly what the Japanese themselves planned, to the point of conserving some 5,000 precious aircraft as the very last line of defense. Boats and aircraft apart, an even more terrifying prospect was outlined in November 1944, requiring every man, woman, and child to participate in *teishin butai* (suicide waves) as the Allied invasion forces came ashore. Intelligence estimates that the war's last invasion could result in a million casualties drove the Americans to seek an alternative and quick end to the war by using a staggering new weapon, the development of which had resulted in a practical test by the spring of 1945.

Top: Dramatic column of smoke after two kamikazes crashed the USS *Bunker Hill* on May 11, 1945. Carriers were the kamikazes' main target, but the *Bunker Hill* survived this inferno.

Above: Enterprise was stuck by a kamikaze on May 24, debris from the explosion hurling what was identified at the time as a section of an aircraft elevator many hundreds of feet above the carrier—which survived the attack.

Right and Above Right: Intrepid was singled out by kamikazes on April 16, 1945, when a "Zeke" fighter crashed the deck near No. 3 elevator and causing substantial damage. Five "Zekes" attempted to crash the carrier, one diving into the sea just as his comrade found the target.

THE MANHATTAN PROJECT

Having assembled an international team of physicists, many of whom had fled Nazi persecution in Europe, the U.S. took up the enormous challenge of funding and building the world's first atomic bomb. Such a bomb, equal in explosive power to millions of tons of TNT, had no defined use at the outset of the top secret Manhattan Project under the command of General Leslie R. Groves. Located far from the nearest habitation at Los Alamos in the Nevada Desert, the bomb development team and its support organization soon grew into a sprawling establishment housing thousands of personnel.

In the laboratories the physicists led by J. Robert Oppenheimer worked to overcome a series of daunting setbacks, including fatal accidents, that dogged the program for many months. Finally, on July 16, 1945, it proved feasible to explode an initial atomic device. The results of the tests, at Alamagordo in New Mexico, were awesome—no weapon had ever released such immense energy in a single chain-reaction. It was now possible to construct an atomic bomb small enough to be carried by a standard AAF bomber. With the war winding down—Germany capitulated on May 8, 1945—but dragging on in the Pacific beyond any reasonable length considering Japan's isolated position, thoughts turned to at least threatening to

use the A-bomb to force the enemy to accept surrender terms.

Harry Truman, who had become president on the death of Franklin Roosevelt, chaired a meeting of the Joint Chiefs of Staff on June 18, to discuss the bomb. Some members felt that, providing that the Japanese were given assurances that their Emperor would not be executed or treated as a war criminal, then they might be persuaded to capitulate without an invasion. This was never done to the satisfaction of the Japanese, with the bomb increasingly becoming the main focus as the quickest way to end hostilities.

A technical demonstration was one of many suggestions to show the power of the bomb without actually harming anyone. Counter views, that the despotic Japanese would merely move Allied prisoners into the designated demonstration zone, were heeded. Given the nature of the enemy, such a move was entirely in character—making the spectre of the carnage a conventional invasion of the home islands would undoubtedly bring an even grimmer nightmare. However, if the Japanese could be shown that the Americans now had the capability of wiping out a major city with a single bomb, then surely the last grains of collective common sense possessed by the enemy leaders would prevail? Nobody could be sure.

Truman informed Churchill of the existence of the bomb at the July Potsdam Conference. The British premier tried, unsuccessfully, to

Above: Ash and aircraft wreckage littered the deck of the *Bunker Hill* after the fires caused by kamikazes had been extinguished.

Left: Aircraft from the British Pacific Fleet made a small but significant contribution to final victory in the Pacific. HMS *Victorious* hit Ishigaki airfield on April 20, 1945, the attack appearing to thoroughly plaster the main runway.

Above Right: Formidable's air group bombed Ishigaki on April 16, these photos showing explosions as the attack developed.

Right: Another frame from the cameras of *Formidable's* strike force during the April attack on Ishigaki.

Left: "We dig them—they fill them," was the original caption to this "before" view of Tokuno airfield after five weeks of U.S. bombing had created over 100 craters. The Japanese did indeed try to keep their airfields open by constantly filling in bomb craters.

Below: Tokuno in an "after" shot which revealed wheeltracks of the trucks used to move earth for filling in craters. The airfield then contained 98 wrecked Japanese aircraft, some of which are visible.

Bottom: HMS *Formidable*'s attack on Ishigaki on April 16 seen just as a wave of Avengers prepares to dive. The British roundel and U.S. national insignia's white bars were combined to create the BPF marking.

Above Right and *Right:* Excellent target photos were brought back of the BPF attack on Ishigaki airfield, a major Japanese base.

persuade Truman to back away from demanding Japan's unconditional surrender, and a proclamation, issued to Japan on July 26, made no mention of the A-bomb, but threatened the country with utter destruction. Neither was any reference made to the fate of the Emperor who had, on June 22, summoned the "big six" to an Imperial Presence Conference to discuss ways of ending the war quickly. In Tokyo, the Potsdam message received a mixed reception; Togo and

Admiral Suzuki supported it, the latter voicing his hope of opening a dialog with the Americans. His ultimate silence, however, was taken by the U.S. as a rejection of the declaration, a view strongly supported by Japanese press comment. Admiral Toda was also opposed, and the U.S. was of the firm opinion that the Japanese would continue to resist.

In the meantime the kamikazes continued to hurl themselves at the fleet off Okinawa. Even as the battle for the island neared its inevitable climax, young pilots, blinded by idealism, climbed aboard their aircraft to poignant and emotion-laden farewells. Each man was presented with a sacred, hand-stitched white scarf, which he wound around his forehead before the time came for take off. As the kamikazes were considered such a select band of pilots—albeit not always very skilled at flying their machines—they were afforded heavy escort by pilots who had the responsibility of warning off American interceptors before returning home.

These mixed formations were tactically sound, in that the Americans were not always able to tell exactly which aircraft were kamikazes. Erratic flying, with little or no evasive action being taken when under attack, could give the game away. Toward the end of the Okinawa campaign, a few of the would-be suiciders changed their minds when they found their attack area covered by cloud or they estimated the situation to be hopeless, but these were the exception.

Planning for using the A-bomb operationally had advanced by late July to the point of using the USS *Indianapolis* to deliver parts of "Little Boy"—the nickname of first A-bomb—to Tinian. Having delivered her cargo the cruiser set sail again, only to be sunk by a Japanese submarine with great loss of life.

Boeing had, in the meantime, modified several B-29s for the special A-bomb delivery mission. With uprated engines and a cleaned up airframe devoid of all gun barbettes, these B-29Bs were faster than standard aircraft. To fly them a new unit, the 509th Composite Group, was sent to Tinian to undertake several conventional bombing missions to gain experience prior to the atomic strike. One of the unit's pilots, Major Paul Tibbets, named the B-29 assigned to him after his mother. After flying a number of missions during the first days of August, the Superfortresses, among them *Enola Gay*, sat baking on their Tinian hardstands, waiting.

SECRET WAR

9. CODE-BREAKING, THE CHINDITS, AND MERRILL'S MARAUDERS

BACKGROUND

Britain had entered the war with a distinct advantage over both the Axis and the United States in terms of technological developments in the military field, particularly radar. A similar situation prevailed in the important area of analysing coded German radio traffic passed by the secret Enigma encoding machine.

Following the early Allied disasters in the Far East, there was firm evidence that the Japanese were far less sophisticated than the Germans in terms of safeguarding their inter-unit communications, and by the time of Pearl Harbor, the U.S. was well on the way to deciphering the content of Japanese diplomatic and military radio messages. An unfortunate series of misunder-

Right: The odyssey of the *Krait* included the establishment of a radio station and coastwatching network. Swimming was one compensation for a nomadic existence.

Below Right: Observation of the movement of Japanese patrols enabled their location and disposition to be passed to Allied military units.

Below: The fishing boat MV *Krait* was a small but vital link in a chain of Allied ships that "cleared up" after major actions. In her case, 1,100 people were carried to safety after the fall of Singapore.

Bottom: Merrill's Marauders fording a jungle stream in northern Burma.

standings and confusion as to the distribution of decoded messages led to no reliable warning being given about the Pearl Harbor attack force—but a few months afterwards the Navy had a very good idea where IJN ships were.

Having established a Combat Intelligence Office under the suitable cryptic designation "Op 20 02," more commonly referred to as "Hypo," the U.S. Navy set out to crack the code used by the Japanese Navy. Known as JN-25, this consisted of about 45,000 five-digit numbers which represented words and phrases. In addition, an even larger set of random numbers could be inserted into messages to deny analysis and the IJN issued books of new codes irregularly.

Along with his team of brilliant individual cryptographers, Commander Joseph Rochefort had painstakingly broken down the IJN code, using little more than applied logic. Working without Japanese code books or decoding machines to give a key to JN-25, Rochefort could by the spring of 1942, read approximately

every fourth or fifth group in each numerical message. From this it became possible for his team to say within a few hundred miles where every ship in the Japanese navy was at any given time.

Rochefort personally never claimed full credit for this service, and the vital work on breaking the Japanese code was always recognized as a team effort. Among others, Admiral Nimitz was highly enthusiastic about the work of Hypo and gave Rochefort a free hand to develop his intelligence service.

Once the United States entered the war, a frantic effort was made to match British methods of decoding, and rapid progress was made. The Americans soon began reading the diplomatic J-19 traffic emanating from Tokyo to missions and embassies sympathetic to the Axis all over the world. Known as "Purple" this material added to an accumulating fund of "Magic" data, this being the codeword for JN-25 decrypts.

Left: Part of the *Krait*'s "passenger list" were members of the crew of HMS *Kuala* who were rescued from the island of Pompong. Basic medical help was also found.

Right: Radio specialists, living off the jungle, sent messages to Allied headquarters warning of Japanese activity.

Below Right: Native villagers were invaluable in helping Allied personnel elude enemy patrols.

GUERILLA FORCES

Right from the outset of the Pacific war the generally atrocious conduct of Japanese troops against native populations and prisoners of war alike created waves of hatred among the people conquered by her armies. Throwing away the chance to recruit thousands of supporters, the Imperial Japanese forces instead brought with them brutal repression, and fostered universal contempt and active opposition in the forms of guerilla groups. These militias, initially fighting with few weapons and scanty provisions were soon fostered, nurtured, and supplied by the main combatants to the point where they became a very real threat to Japanese Army operations throughout Southeast Asia. Using the local knowledge supplied by natives desperate to rid their country of the "common enemy," the Allies gradually built up a fund of intelligence material vital for future campaigns.

Many Allied aircrew (men particularly at risk if they were captured) were saved by friendly tribes chagrined at their treatment at the hands of the invaders; in areas such as New Guinea, teams of coastwatchers maintained a continual, clandestine surveillance of enemy movements and strength. These individuals were particularly adept at providing early warning of Japanese air attacks; in a theater that lacked modern airborne early warning equipment such as ground radar this information, passed along a network of watchers, proved the difference between Allied aircraft getting off the ground in time or being destroyed on their airfields.

While they were attempting to suppress—usually by coercion and outright force—thousands of civilians captured in their early war campaigns, the Japanese had to cope with the constant demands of their original war theater, China. American power and influence, far exceeding those of the Japanese, were wielded freely to secure cooperation and practical help to fight the common enemy. This influence spread to India, Burma, and many areas of China which traditionally had few dealings with the United States.

While the hard currency pumped into U.S. bases overseas profited local traders and impoverished populations in numerous areas, on a wider canvas U.S. diplomatic efforts successfully persuaded individuals such as Mao Tse Tung of the Communist Chinese to align himself with

Chiang Kai-shek's Nationalists, at least until the Japanese were beaten. These positive efforts added to a gratifying pro-Allied stance which was vital in many areas dominated by the enemy. Once convinced that the Japanese would ultimately be forced to leave their country, local communities often needed little further persuasion to join the Allied cause and serve it in a host of roles, however small these may have been. Active service attracted enough individuals to represent a significant threat to the Japanese and one that they could hardly ignore.

To exploit this the Allies raised a number of clandestine groups and trained them specifically to operate behind Japanese lines. Mainly offshoots of existing organizations such as the British Special Operations Executive (SOE) and the U.S. Office of Strategic Services (OSS), the *raison d'être* of these small, well-armed, and well-equipped groups was to operate as far as was practicable behind enemy lines, and to harass and disrupt Japanese communications, destroy dumps, airfields, and transport, and to wipe out pockets of troops.

Although aiming to be generally self-sustaining these guerillas or long-range penetration groups were supplied by air whenever possible

Above: A grim reminder of what the Allies were fighting in the Far East. This Japanese truck, knocked out by grenades during Operation "Otter," was decorated by the skulls of enemy dead.

Left: The superlative de Havilland Mosquito was a latecomer to the Far East war, but it made its mark there as much as in other theaters. On March 29, 1945, No. 45 Squadron aircraft hit a suspension bridge on the Hopong–Kemapyu road, broke the cables, and dropped the central span into the river.

Below Left: Although the Japanese threw a causeway across the river No. 45's Mosquitos paid it another visit on May 11, the aircrews claiming hits on it.

Above Right: Bilin was one of many targets in Burma attacked by No. 159 Squadron's Liberators on June 8, 1945.

but an initial shortage of transport aircraft often militated against this, resulting in some groups being virtually cut off for months and obliged to live off the land as best they could.

Among the most colorful of these forces were the Chindits, founded by Major Orde Wingate, who was no stranger to controversy in the British military establishment because of his unconventional approach to war. No enthusiastic supporter of what were derisively termed "private armies," the British Army officially frowned on units such as those pioneered by David Stirling of the Long Range Desert Group, the forerunner of the SAS—and Orde Wingate.

This view was shared by Bill Slim who, while acknowledging the courage of the Chindits, viewed what later came to be termed special forces as "expensive, wasteful, and unnecessary." Among his objections to such formations was that, unlike regular troops, the specialists were generally trained for only one type of operation, and they had to be periodically brought out of the jungle to recoup. Slim was also against the cult of the elite, the attraction for extrovert characters to win a little glory, and that they were—again in contrast to line troops—better

equipped by having first call on the best weapons Fortunately for such passionate characters, their ideas appealed to the romantic in Churchill. In 1945 he approved of Stirling's plan to send 2 SAS Regiment to operate in China, an event curtailed by the atomic bombs.

Wingate, however, prevailed, with his Chindits becoming perhaps the best known of the clandestine units to operate in Burma. A firm believer in the modestly sized, self-sustaining force able to exist behind enemy lines for months on end, Wingate's view did not gain much official support until after his first campaign was completed.

The Chindits' second, and most ambitious, operation was undertaken in parallel with that of the Fourteenth Army's offensive in 1944. Having become more of a regular, much-expanded force after Orde Wingate's death in an air crash on March 24, the Chindits were organized more along army lines. This was an eventuality that Wingate had anticipated but resisted as far as possible; his view was that the individuality and flexibility of his troops would be compromised if military regulations were imposed upon them. Such changes were, nevertheless, made after his death.

Making their jumping off point for the first major Burma operation the secret landing strip of "Broadway," the Chindits were led by Wingate himself. Thinking nothing of riding with the mules in the back of a Dakota if a cot was unavailable, the bearded, pith-helmeted Wingate cut an unmistakeable figure among the more conventionally attired Army officers.

Among the guerillas recruited by the OSS to fight the Japanese in Indo-Chia was one Ho Chi Minh. An enthusiastic supporter of the Allied cause, Ho and individuals like him were convinced that once the Japanese had been defeated their efforts would be rewarded by an end to colonial rule—about which Ho was equally passionate. His guerillas were supplied well by the Americans.

It was, perhaps, unfortunate that men like Ho Chi Minh were cast into something of a void when the Americans quickly left Southeast Asia in 1945. Into that void stepped representatives of the old colonial powers—the French, British, and Dutch. This was the last thing that the nationalist groups wanted. As soon as they realized that the powerful wartime Allies had little intention of changing the status quo, much less of giving away their colonies, Ho and others like him began to realize, however reluctantly, that resorting to military force was the only answer.

An outgrowth of the long-range guerilla band pioneered by Orde Wingate was the U.S.-originated commando group officially designated the 5307th Composite Unit (Provisional), a regimental-size formation known more popularly as "Merrill's Marauders." That title came later, however; locally called "Galahad" force, these Americans trained with and accompanied Wingate's early forays and adopted his basic unit structure of dividing each battalion into "columns." Not all Americans officers—many of whom were cool towards the whole Burma campaign—agreed with this approach, but Stilwell, aware of the need to prove that U.S. troops were committed to Burma's liberation as much as the British, desired some tangible results. Galahad force accepted the fact that they might well be cast as role models to the Chinese, who initially showed some reluctance in fighting the Japanese. For their part the Marauders were chagrined at the prospect of extended combat tours when they had been promised rotation to the U.S. after only three months in the field.

Below: Mosquitos look over the Japanese HQ at Myohle on March 31, 1945, prior to the main attack taking place.

LORRY ATTACKED AND LEFT ABLAZE
Position: MUANG PHAN

To Accompany P.I.R. A/30

Above Left: Much of the Burma air effort was a "war of the rails" to deny the Japanese their supplies. This massive explosion on a train plying the Bangkok–Singapore line surely indicated the end of an ammunition car.

Above and Left: Allied aircraft were even hunting individual trucks as Japanese forces pulled out of Burma. This attack (Left) on one on the Lampang–Chiengrai road on November 11, 1944, was typical of hundreds.

Stilwell need not have worried unduly. Ably led by Brig-Gen. Frank D. Merrill, the force, in concert with the Chinese, made contact with the Japanese 18th Division at Maingkwan during March 1944. Then commanded by General Tanaka, the Japanese division only just managed to extricate itself before it was totally destroyed. Tanaka would not be caught off guard again. He not only eluded the Marauders during a second sweep they conducted into the jungle between March 28 and April 1, but at one point he threatened to overrun the American positions before air and ground forces were able to break the deadlock. This was fortunate, for when the Japanese began besieging Imphal and Kohima, they threatened not only the British Fourteenth Army but the U.S. Tenth Air Force bases which were largely responsible for supplying the Marauders.

The modest U.S. ground effort in northern Burma was increasingly dwarfed by the contribution of the Chinese Army. Stilwell welcomed two more Chinese divisions and meanwhile sent his two original divisions, the 22nd and 38th, into Mogaung Valley with the object of capturing Myitkyina airfield before the start of the monsoon. This airfield harbored the Japanese fighters well placed to attack the transports flying the Hump route and removing that threat

Above: Allied agents were dropped into the enemy-held jungle virtually throughout the war. As this group with a workhorse Lysander shows, dress, particularly that of native carriers, was often quite informal!

would help ensure the Marauders' supplies were not curtailed.

Well equipped and trained, the Chinese troops nevertheless found that the jungles of Burma represented numerous challenges to any group attempting to penetrate its heart. Even with the tide turning against Japan, Merrill's forces suffered casualties, not all of which were as a result of enemy action. The Chinese 30th Division, some 7,000 men strong, began traversing some very tough country to reach Myitkyina airfield. This they did on May 17.

Although the airfield was secure enough to allow RAF reinforcement flights to use it, the following day's attack on Myitkyina town—served by the notorious Burma Railway which Allied PoWs were then extending to Bangkok—was over ambitious. The Marauders were repulsed by a small Japanese garrison force and, riven by disease, took heavy casualties. Tanaka, not fully appreciating his numerical superiority at the start of the battle, now found freshly arrived Chinese troops behind him. Shaking off this threat with typical coolness, Tanaka counter-attacked with all the troops he could muster from his own 18th Division and other units. However, the Chinese in their turn repulsed all these assaults and began to wear down the Japanese by mounting their own counter-offensives.

The Chindits, meanwhile, had been forced to abandon their railway blockade at "Blackpool," and on May 17 pulled back into the mountains at Kamaing. Expecting to be relieved, they were instead urged into action again by Maj-Gen. Lentaigne at the behest of Stilwell. They were needed to pinch off the left flank of the Japanese 18th Division.

Tanaka remained calm in adversity, and continued to withstand the Chinese even as he was forced to retreat. Then the Chindit 77th Brigade cut across his lines and proceeded to indulge in the kind of pitched battle that Wingate had never sought for his force.

Nevertheless, this battle was won and Tanaka finally conceded Mogaung; Myitkyina was subjected to an increasingly effective Allied blockade, but the Japanese continued to receive supplies and reinforcements via a corridor across the Irrawaddy. Surrounded by huge numbers of Chinese troops, Tanaka continued to hold out, repulsing numerous attacks on his positions and even withstanding artillery barrages.

Merrill's Marauders, their three months of combat now expired, were adamant about being withdrawn. Looking askance at the low morale and weakened state of the Americans, Stilwell, against his own better judgement, complied. All was not, however, lost as Stilwell retained a cadre of Marauder survivors to create a new Marauder force known as "New Galahad." Thrown back into the battle for Myitkyina, these newcomers helped bolster the morale of the Chinese, who continued to fight well despite the early doubts of their leaders that their troops lacked the necessary will to survive harsh conditions and a tough enemy.

It took the Allies more than eleven weeks to secure Myitkyina. When Tokyo finally ordered Tanaka to conduct an orderly withdrawal, he accomplished this with about 600 of his men, the incredibly courageous Japanese defense being the hallmark of the campaign. Less honor was afforded the U.S. and British Chindits, who true to their "three months" creed all but collapsed after their allocated time in combat had expired. Their record was in marked contrast to that of the Japanese, who in this operation at least relinquished none of their reputation as the world's finest jungle fighters.

Thus the battle for Burma drew to a close. Orde Wingate's original concept of LRP brigades was certainly vindicated—but with him gone, the nature of the force changed. It was said, with some justification, by his British colleagues that he overstated the effectiveness of his force against a numerically superior enemy to the point where they lost the initiative. Surprisingly, the Japanese thought otherwise. They deployed massive forces trying to hunt down the elusive guerillas and this undoubtedly had an adverse effect, not only on their ability to mount pitched battles but on the morale of the rank and file troops, who never knew when the guerrillas were going to strike next.

In summary, the clandestine activities of a number of Allied guerilla and commando groups materially helped to bring about the downfall of the Japanese Army in Burma. Having invariably taken terrible casualties in pitched battles with regular Allied units, the Japanese tended to melt away into the jungle to regroup. Harassed by Allied commando units and all but cut off from their supply lines, heavily interdicted by Allied sea and airpower, Imperial troops enjoyed nothing like the degree of aerial resupply that succored their opponents. For transport of their supplies, Japanese soldiers were driven to rely most heavily on river traffic, but this too was attacked with a relentless ferocity.

Having often been broken into piecemeal, relatively ineffective small groups, Japanese units were, by 1945, forced to live off the often meager resources of the jungle. In spite of their legendary ability to exist on a few daily grains of rice, even the Japanese could not expect to remain effective on starvation rations for protracted periods. There was a degree of local assistance from the Burmese, although—as has already been discussed—the army's generally brutal behavior often denied Japanese troops the vital help native tribes might otherwise have provided. Despite this, the net result was that regular Imperial Army units, decimated by battle casualties and disease, withered away to a shadow of their former strength and were ultimately forced to surrender through starvation and a total lack of the means to fight, rather than any lessening of morale—although by the spring of 1945 this, too, was starting to wane.

FIRE OVER NIPPON

10. DOOLITTLE, BOMBING JAPAN, HIROSHIMA AND NAGASAKI

THE DOOLITTLE RAID

In early 1942, in an effort to strike back at Japan after the previous months of near-total military disaster, Roosevelt and his main military advisors—including the chief of the USAAF, General "Hap" Arnold, and the C-in-C of the Navy, Admiral Ernest King—agreed that a major coup was needed. The result was a risky plan to bomb targets in Japan by aircraft launched from an aircraft carrier. Bombing the Japanese homeland would create a huge propaganda victory for the United States, one that the enemy would be hard put to live down. Immense loss of face would result.

A strike by conventional carrier-borne aircraft, though feasible, could not deliver the weight of ordnance such a raid required. The

compromise of using Army bombers, which would fly on to land bases in China after the mission, was greeted with widespread enthusiasm by the select circle of high-ranking officers involved in the project. The Army's bombers could deliver a substantial weight of explosive and, by achieving total surprise, they could escape before the enemy knew what had hit him.

So it was to prove. After examining the alternatives, the only aircraft able to take off from a carrier deck, carry a substantial bomb load, and, with extra fuel, reach Tokyo from the nearest designated point to Japan, was the North American B-25 Mitchell. The raid was to be led by Colonel (later lieutenant-general) "Jimmy" Doolittle, who set about planning the operation in the minutest detail. Being unable to tell anyone the target, Doolittle shouldered great responsibility; not everyone understood his

urgency to have the B-25s thoroughly inspected and modified where necessary. Training for the mission was also compromised for much the same reason, as crews strove to lift their B-25Bs off runways marked out to the dimensions of a carrier deck.

Perseverance paid off, and Doolittle finally oversaw the loading of his bombers aboard U.S. Navy carrier *Hornet* in late March 1942. On April 1, without ceremony, *Hornet* slipped her moorings in San Francisco and headed for a rendezvous with USS *Enterprise* and the small carrier task force bound for the Japanese home islands under Commander (later Admiral) Bill Halsey.

Spotted by Japanese picket boats in the early hours of April 18, the force had to launch the bombers early and the last Mitchell left the *Hornet* over 500 miles from Japan. This meant that, after bombing, the Army crews would be unlikely to reach China before darkness fell.

Left and Right: The B-25s dwarfed the *Hornet*'s flightdeck as they traveled towards Japan. Taking off from a pitching carrier deck was a dangerous affair, but all managed it safely.

Finding airfields in unfamiliar terrain in the dark was a daunting prospect that resulted in the loss of all but one of the B-25s through crash landings and crews opting to bail out rather than risk flying into mountains they could not see. The sole exception was a crew that headed for Russia to make a safe landing.

The raiders duly arrived over an unsuspecting Tokyo at around 14.00 local time, and released their bombs, to the delight of the B-25 crews and the naval personnel who had delivered them there. Screams of rage and confusion could be heard over the radio as the American task force withdrew.

Choosing their briefed targets without difficulty the bulk of the Mitchell force swept across the enemy capital. There was some opposition but interceptor fighters were too late to catch them and AAA fire was erratic and inaccurate. Other bombers targeted Yokohama and Yokosuka. All of them dropped their loads and headed toward China, except for one that went north and landed at Vladivostok. Of the 80 or so men involved in the raid, eight were captured and four killed, although a number of those captured were later executed.

The results were impressive: on the verge of hysteria, the Japanese high command ordered that the defenses of Tokyo be considerably strengthened. From that moment on, the Japanese had cause to fear that their cities might once again come under attack from enemy bombers. This prospect had been so unexpected before the raid that unsuspecting citizens had waved to the American aircraft. Doolittle's small force caused more consternation than actual damage in the capital, but the strategic result was positive. In an effort to ensure that such a raid could not happen again, the Japanese set in motion plans that would lead to the great carrier battles of 1942 (see Chapter 3).

Mitchells were unable to return to Tokyo until 1945; the AAF was not about to attempt another carrier launch with bombers and, until the war moved much closer to Japan, twin-engined aircraft did not have the necessary range.

BOMBING JAPAN

By the autumn of 1944, Japan's military position in the Southwest and Central Pacific was little short of dire. Given that the United States was unlikely to stop its overwhelming air and sea operations until its troops were fighting in the streets of Tokyo, Japan could only pull back and keep pulling back to the home islands. Unless Japan surrendered the U.S. expected to mount a bloody invasion, Operation "Olympic," in the spring of 1946.

In the meantime a wholesale assault on Japan from the air was planned. Each major Japanese city containing industries important to the war effort would be attacked by a force of very long-range bombers. Inevitably, those areas surrounding the factories would not escape the rain of bombs, but justification for what had in Europe been termed "area" rather than the traditional American "precision" bombing was that the Japanese had also turned many suburbs of their major cities into miniature war production centers, with small groups constructing a myriad of parts for military equipment of all kinds. More obviously, killing the workers who manned the factories would, it was assumed, have a further detrimental effect on output and morale. Japanese civilian dwellings were far less robustly built than those in Germany, making them highly susceptible to destruction by incendiary attack. Fire raids would be far more effective than they had ever been in Europe.

It was, nevertheless, a prerequisite of the bomber offensive that the aiming points for the crews would invariably be factories, particularly those associated with Japan's aero industry at all levels—airframes, engines, and production lines. It was further decided that a new bomber, the Boeing B-29 Superfortress, successor to the famous B-17 Fortress, would be used to undertake the campaign.

Building the B-29 in quantity gave Boeing numerous problems that delayed the entry of the aircraft into AAF service, but when the output from the giant plants at Renton and Wichita had been better integrated with AAF modification centers, the aircraft was ready for service. This began in April 1944, well in time to take the war to the enemy. So different was the B-29 program to anything that had gone before that a new Army Air Force, the 20th, was created to operate it.

At first the 20th Bomber Command was organized on proven, conventional lines; aircraft bombing altitudes (20,000-30,000ft) would be similar to those adopted successfully by the strategic air forces in Europe, and the Superforts would fly in formation to make maximum use of their defensive firepower to ward off the attentions of enemy fighters. Among its modern innovations, the B-29 was given a remotely-controlled defensive system under which gunners aimed their weapons from sighting stations divorced from the gun barbettes.

It was decided that bases in the CBI (Chine-Burma-India) operational area would be most suitable for the B-29s, and accordingly a number of bases were established on the Ganges plain, some 70 miles west of Calcutta. The first four operational groups (constituting one wing) of B-29s moved into their Indian bases in the spring of 1944, and the initial campaign got underway on June 5, when 48 aircraft bombed Bangkok by radar due to heavy undercast.

These missions—hampered by the need to haul every bomb and gallon of fuel across the Hump route to forward operating bases in China—continued for some six months. They failed to deliver the kind of intensive aerial assault that AAF planners had hoped would knock Japan out of the war in double quick time. It was through no fault of the early

Superfortress crews that a decision was taken to move the bomber bases out to the Marianas, where access to supplies by air and sea was infinitely better.

While they had flown bombing missions from the CBI Theater, the B-29 groups had also conducted an extensive mining campaign, one that particularly impressed the SEAC C-in-C. Mountbatten felt that rendering the sea lanes highly dangerous to shipping was a significant factor in speeding Japan's defeat. This view was reinforced by the cripplingly high tonnage lost to mines in the last year of the war.

Under the command of Brig-Gen. Haywood "Possum" Hansell, 21st Bomber Command reflexed its muscles in the Marianas. All the bomber conventions thoroughly learned in Europe were followed as the B-29 opened a second phase of the campaign against the home islands.

When his command moved to Saipan, Hansell and others had largely to estimate the extent of the Japanese defenses, although the number of AAA guns and interceptor fighters were not believed to equal the scale of those surrounding German targets. Each B-29, nevertheless, took off from its Marianas base with a full complement of ammunition for its guns which, together with a maximum fuel load, made for a very heavy 135,000lb aircraft. Bomb loads had to be trimmed accordingly, with few aircraft being able to carry the maximum 20,000lb.

Fuel would, of course, be progressively burned to lighten the aircraft during the flight to the target, but it was still a long haul. Japan represented a 3,000-mile round trip from Tinian, most of it over an ocean which experienced some of the worst weather in the world. Crews soon became aware of how rapidly conditions could change. Flying in bright sunshine one moment, they would find mists suddenly developing to blot out even the largest reference point in the largely featureless expanse of the Pacific. Winds could take an aircraft miles off track in a very short time, and the violence of multiple thunderstorms experienced five miles above Japan was a wonder to behold. Cloud often hampered bombing at high altitude over the

Left: Complete photo coverage of the major targets in Japan included this February 17, 1945, view of the airfield at Hyakurigahara with more than a dozen revetments containing aircraft.

Left: The Japanese learned to disperse their combat aircraft well away from the main runway and buildings of airfields. Typical widespread dispersal shows up on this view of Hyakurigahara.

Right: More widely dispersed aircraft visible on Takahagi airfield northeast of Tokyo on 10 July 1945.

Far Right: Takahagi's hangars and other installations being worked over by aircraft of TF-58.3 on February 16, 1945.

target areas, the Japanese islands often being completely obscured.

Following several shakedown missions to Truk and Iwo Jima, the first mission to the Empire was launched from Tinian on November 24, 1944. Tokyo was, appropriately enough, the chosen target, Nakajima's aero engine assembly plant at Musashino being the specific objective under a plan to neutralize the enemy's aircraft industry.

Take off was just after dawn. The lead bombers were above Tokyo by midday and apart from the F-13s (the photographic version of the B-29) that preceded the mission, these were the first enemy aircraft to appear over the city since the Doolittle raid some 31 months previously.

Yet the results of the first B-29 raid on Tokyo were disappointing, as were the subsequent precision attacks on such locations as Nagoya and Ota, which lasted through January 1945. The B-29s maintained the pressure, with varying numbers of aircraft attacking at night and raiding targets of opportunity by day when the number of available aircraft could not constitute a major strike. One hundred was the optimum number desired by Washington, and Hansell did

what he could to put this number over the target, coping with aircraft needing repair, Japanese fighter attacks on his bases and missions being scrubbed through adverse weather conditions. He was not yet able to send off 100 B-29s as the strength of one Superfort wing was four groups, a nominal total of around 75 aircraft.

On these early missions HE bombs, incendiaries, and parafrags were dropped, but what with aircraft turning back with technical faults, quite heavy fighter opposition—the results of which were boosted by the enemy's penchant for deliberately ramming the big bombers—flak and weather, the period was frustrating.

The long haul back from Japan also meant a steady number of damaged B-29s having to ditch long before they reached their home airfields. The subsequent capture of Iwo Jima to serve as a "halfway house" between the Marianas and Japan did not remove the need for an efficient rescue organization. The volcanic island was often "socked in" by cloud, obliging crews to make water landings but they were at least closer to help after the island was in U.S. hands.

Picking up downed B-29 crews was a problem addressed quickly, and a network of Navy submarines, ships, and B-29 "Super Dumbos"—

Superforts equipped with liferafts, medical, and food supplies for parachuting to survivors—was organized. The Super Dumbos were named after the original Dumbos, the shorter ranged Catalina flying boats, and the name became generic for any rescue aircraft. These B-29s performed a vital task and, although they could not of course land on water, numerous crewmen were saved by their diligent search efforts.

All things considered, the early B-29 bombing campaign from the Marianas was not bringing the results desired by Washington quickly enough; the priority target list was being worked through, but reconnaissance showed that specific factories were not being destroyed, necessitating repeat missions to "finish the job." By no yardstick could the results be described as spectacular.

Hap Arnold laid part of the problem with the B-29 campaign at the door of its commander—"Possum" Hansell. He moved quickly and appointed Curtis LeMay to take over 21st Bomber Command, effective late January 1945. Arnold felt LeMay to be more flexible than Hansell—but the same problems remained to be solved.

LEMAY'S GAMBLE

LeMay himself had ample experience—in Europe—of what could result when bombers challenged defenses that had already been alerted, but this was not Europe. Here, the B-29s tended to fly so high that Japanese fighter interception was often difficult; indeed, some of the defending fighters were obliged to operate at the virtual limit of their service ceiling. Flak, however, was able to reach the bombers and it was accurate enough to cause considerable damage, even when it did not bring bombers down.

By studying the patchy results achieved to date given the nature of the relatively light structures his bombers were aiming to knock out, LeMay realized that something was wrong. He also noted that, although these early raids were unescorted, bomber losses were nowhere near as heavy as they had been in Europe in the early stages of the campaign from England.

With a free hand to act as he saw fit, LeMay took a huge risk. He ordered the crews to strip their aircraft of anything to save weight including many defensive guns, to carry incendiaries

Above: During the last months of the war targets in Japan were attacked whenever weather permitted. On February 17, 1945, it was the turn of the Tachikawa engine plant in the Tokyo area.

rather than HE bombs—and then to go over the target at less than 10,000ft—and at night.

Drastic was the mildest word the crews used for their new commander's plan, but they had little choice but to comply. Who could tell if the new tactics would work? The answer soon came: during the afternoon of March 9, 1945, 334 B-29s began taking off from all three bases in the Marianas. Late that evening Tokyo's airspace was penetrated by 282 bombers, with pathfinders creating a literal cross of fire in the city as an aiming point. Just after midnight, the 73rd Wing completed its bomb run and the 500lb clusters of M-69 incendiary bombs released by each B-29 cascaded toward the Japanese capital. Searchlights probed for the bombers and the flak began, but the first fires were taking hold. Fanned by a high wind which struck the city just before the first bombs fell, the fires spread, grew in intensity, then joined with others. Roaring walls of flame destroyed everything in their path—people, houses, bridges, vehicles and supplies of all kinds were consumed. Fire fighters were swamped when much of their equipment burned and the intense heat made the very rivers boil.

LeMay's gamble had paid off with a vengeance. The great Tokyo fire raid destroyed 15.8 square miles of built-up area and claimed the lives of some 78,600 people, according to Japanese figures. The cost had been 14 B-29s lost and 40 more with varying degrees of damage.

LeMay piled on the pressure—Nagoya was attacked on March 11 with less spectacular results than Tokyo, as no wind helped fan the flames; then eight square miles of Osaka were razed on the 13th. Kobe's turn came on March 16, when 307 B-29s burned out a fifth of the city. Finally the LeMay blitz fell once again on Nagoya, which lost another three square miles.

These five missions had accomplished more in terms of damage than all previous Superfortress raids, leaving the dazed Japanese trying to comprehend the enormity of the death toll, and the devastation across 32 square miles of dwellings and factories in four of her principal cities. The defenses had signally failed to ward off the big bombers, and the war leaders had no practical answer—they had no reason other than to fear that this was just the start.

Night raids on Japan indeed continued to yield variable results, the most significant block to success remaining the weather. Danger to the bomber crews also came via their own efforts; huge boiling clouds of super-heated smoke

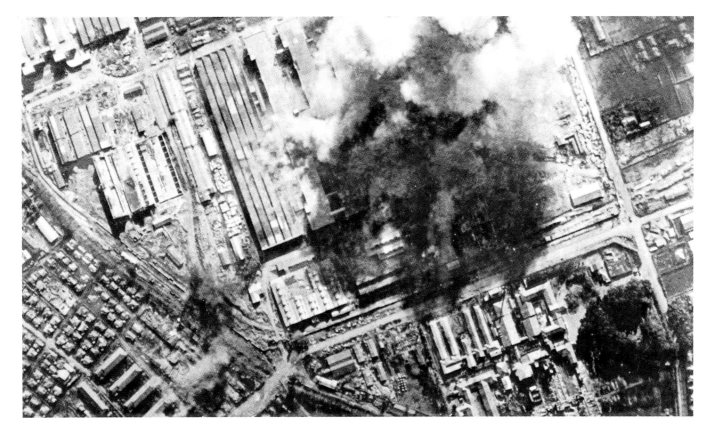

Above: More than 100 of TF 58.3's aircraft bombed the Musashino engine plant in metropolitan Tokyo on February 17, 1945. It was estimated that this plant supplied engines for some 40% of all enemy aircraft.

Left: Task Group 58.3 hit the "power houses" of the Koizumi plant on February 25, 1945, the aiming point for a deluge of 1,000 and 500lb bombs being the important Nakajima airframe assembly buildings.

Below Left: TBF Avengers from *Essex* over Tokyo en route to attack the Nakajima plant situated on the outskirts of the city on February 25, 1945.

created by target fires were quite capable of flipping a Superfort over on its back or hurling one aircraft uncontrollably into another, and the stories of narrow escapes from death and injury by many participating crewmen were legion. Such were risks the crews accepted.

Interspersing their bombing missions with mining sorties, the B-29 force continued to focus their bomb aiming points on aircraft and engine production and component supply centers in the various cities. Already hard put to keep pace with the rate of combat and training losses, Japan's aircraft industry was struggling to build enough airframes and engines to supply the forces in the field, defend the country, and maintain a training schedule. The American knew that if such output could be drastically curtailed at source the already eclipsed JAAF and JNAF could be virtually annihilated.

Left: A photo that reflects near-total U.S. dominance of Japanese airspace in 1945 shows a relatively slow TBF Avenger from *Essex* droning directly over Tsukuba airfield en route to attack the Ota airframe assembly plant.

Below: Mopping up the remnants of the Japanese fleet, the destroyer USS *Haynsworth* shelled enemy picket boats off Tokyo on February 16, 1945. Survivors were passed to the carrier USS *Essex.*

Below Right: At Kure the last capital ships of the IJN largely succumbed to overwhelming air attack. The victims included the *Hyuga* partially converted as a carrier with a flight deck aft.

One of the most urgent requirements, that of reducing the number of in-service kamikazes attacking Navy ships, was next to impossible to achieve by bombing factories. In spite of systematically wiping out Japanese industry in city after city, the B-29 campaign appeared to yield little in the way of positive moves by the enemy to negotiate peace. Proud to a point beyond all reason, the warlords held out, harboring the notion of wiping out the Allied invasion as and when it took place, by mass kamikaze attack.

DOUBLE DEVASTATION

The U.S. was equally well aware that such was almost certainly the Japanese intention. Although Japanese peace feelers were received, no practical steps were actually taken by the enemy, and the clock moved steadily towards the date of the first A-bomb strike. By late July 1945 the target list for the 20th Air Force was moving down towards Hiroshima, and it was that city which was selected for what was fervently hoped would be the only such demonstration of the power of the new bomb.

Paul Tibbets had proven himself one of the top pilots in the crack 509th Group and his aircraft was designated to carry the atomic bomb. The group had trained to a peak of efficiency far

outweighing those of other Superfort wings. Combat missions prior to the atomic strike had shown that this prowess yielded "excellent" bombing results without any losses of personnel or aircraft.

Loading the weapon was something of a challenge—not through weight but bulk. The solution was simply to dig a pit, lower the bomb ("Little Boy") into it and taxi *Enola Gay*—named after Tibbets' mother—over its payload.

By August 1, 1945, the 509th was awaiting the order to fly the mission that would end the war and usher in a new age. Only the weather held things up. The bomb had to be dropped visually and the forecast, previously gloomy, then looked good for the week of August 5–10. The raid was set for the 6th.

On August 2, a major reorganisation of the 20th Air Force saw Curtis LeMay appointed Chief of Staff with General Nathan Twining taking over command of the B-29s in the Marianas. General Carl "Tooey" Spaatz was placed in overall command of a U.S. Strategic Air Forces organization, headquartered on Guam, and similar to that established in Europe. In the meantime the largest B-29 mission of the war took place on August 1 when 851 aircraft were sent against a variety of targets in Japan.

Hiroshima, previously spared the attention of the regular B-29 force, was gaining a reputation as a "safe" city. The Japanese could not know that the city was deliberately being avoided after having been placed on a list of four cities—with Kyoto, Niigata, and Kokura—selected for the atomic attack. Nagasaki, not actually considered an ideal target, was added later. All five were then set aside by the U.S. bombers as an undamaged city was required for accurate damage assessment when the A-bomb exploded.

Although Tibbets' aircraft was obviously the most important the first atomic strike was not to be a lone aircraft sortie. A number of B-29s were to take off from Tinian on August 6, the small force comprising camera aircraft to record the

Above: A scene of Hiroshima after the bomb. The domed building in the center was preserved as a shrine to the city's dead.

Below: A crossroads at the center of Hiroshima, surrounded by the irradiated ash of thousands of dwellings.

Right: Bomb damage plot of Nagasaki. From a 1,000ft circle covering ground-zero (the point of impact) the distances are measured in 2,000ft radiating circles.

Below Right: Hiroshima scene looking toward the impact point. U.S. assessors labeled each standing building in the city to measure the effects of blast. In the foreground, building 40 has a dished roof complete with accumulated water.

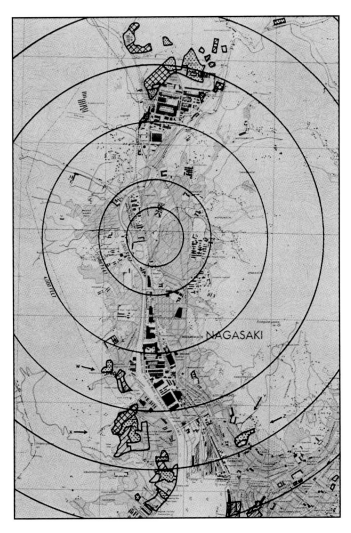

detonation and rescue machines, the "Super Dumbos" crammed with liferafts and other gear to sustain aircrew in the event of a ditching.

On the morning of the 6th Paul Tibbets and his crew boarded their aircraft and took off from Tinian in company with the weather recon and photographic B-29s. The flight was routine; few other Allied aircraft were up that day, although there were some fighter pilot witnesses to what happened, flying a suitable distance away.

As the A-bomb exploded, Tibbets and his crew knew they had released an incredible weapon: nothing like it had ever been dropped in anger by any other bomber in history. Donning protective glasses to shield their eyes from the flash of the bomb, the crew of the *Enola Gay* turned for home.

Anticipating an immediate response to the devastation of Hiroshima, the U.S. government was amazed that no word was received from Tokyo; to ram home the point, the second strike against Nagasaki was ordered for August 8. Again a named B-29—*Bock's Car*—made a long climb out of Tinian with its deadly cargo. This bomb, shaped more conventionally than the rotund Hiroshima weapon, was named "Fat Man" Although pilot Major Charles Sweeney

encountered some haze over the target, conditions were clear enough for him to bomb. The effect was much the same as over Hiroshima.

Even as the characteristic mushroom cloud over Nagasaki dispersed, the war went on. Everyone had hoped that it would take a matter of hours for the Japanese to agree to capitulate, but it was August 10 before anything definite was received. Two days beforehand, the Soviet Union declared war on Japan.

Unsure as to developments at a political level, Spaatz was advised to continue small scale B-29 raids. President Truman halted them on August 11, but ordered resumption on the 14th. In the meantime the third and fourth atomic bombs were being readied for use.

Finally, in what turned out to be a grand finale, over 800 B-29s were launched against eight different targets on the night of August 14/15. There were no combat losses, and before

Above: Mushroom cloud above Nagasaki. Used to force Japan to surrender and save the lives that would be lost in an invasion of the Japanese homeland, the atomic bombs finally brought to an end the Pacific war.

Above Left: The main rail line through Nagasaki flanked by complete destruction. Only the strongest buildings survived the atomic blast.

Left: View of Nagasaki showing the degree of devastation from the atomic bomb blast.

the last of the participating crews had returned to the Marianas, Truman had announced the unconditional surrender of Japan.

In some 14 months of combat operations B-29s dropped nearly 170,000 tons of bombs on Japan and laid 12,000 mines in enemy waters in over 34,000 effective sorties. On the debit side, 147 B-29s had been lost in combat from an overall total of 414 aircraft, and 3,015 crewmen had been killed, wounded or were missing.

The Boeing B-29 Superfortress had been one of the most feared weapons the Japanese had

been faced with, and the two atomic strikes plus the devastating fire raids on Tokyo, had convinced even the diehards that their cause was utterly lost. B-29 mining operations had also materially assisted the widespread sinking of shipping in home waters and the resulting loss of vital food supplies; many Japanese were literally starving by the time of the surrender. Soon after that event the Superforts became harbingers not of death but life, as their crews flew many peaceful sorties to locate hundreds of camps housing Allied PoWs.

By the time hostilities ceased, the surviving inmates of many camps were desperately in need of food and medical supplies. British, American, Canadian, Australian and New Zealand troops made up the majority of the 95,134 PoWs in Japanese hands at the end of the war. Many of these were in an emaciated and diseased state upon release, and in percentage terms, 28.65 out of every 100 men had died, the majority of them having been killed as a result of brutal treatment, untreated wounds, or disease.

CONCLUSION

WAR CRIMES, MANCHURIA, AND THE RECKONING

The catalog of atrocities against prisoners of the Japanese made grim reading when many of the main perpetrators of such acts were tried and convicted at a tribunal held in Tokyo under presiding judge William Webb in May 1946. Sentenced to death for his part in guiding the country's disastrous war, Tojo was one of 900 so condemned and the only Axis head of state to be executed by the Allies. These deliberations tended to overshadow the fact that the rank and file Japanese soldier had displayed admirable courage and skill in battle. He was one of the toughest adversaries the Allies had to face anywhere, and he continued to fight hard even under appalling conditions, when the supply situation was critical and only starvation-level rations remained.

Below and Above Right: The view from an attacking aircraft as Kure Harbor comes under fire.

The Japanese Army, having suffered terrible casualties on the Pacific battlefields, was to lose more men before the final curtain. Just as Japan was on the point of ending hostilities, the Russians had declared war.

STALIN'S END RUN

When Russia invaded Manchuria on August 8, Stalin's aim was to wipe out the shame of the 1905 seizure of Port Arthur by the Japanese. Facing the Japanese-manned Kwantung Army which had guarded the frontier with Soviet Russia and Mongolia throughout WWII, the Red Army mustered a strength of 1,500,000 men, 5,500 tanks, and 3,900 aircraft. Opposing the Russians were over one million Japanese troops with 1,155 tanks and 1,800 aircraft.

Not about to lose this campaign, which held the prize of important territorial gains, Stalin

replaced most of his Far Eastern army and corps commanders with men who had seen action in Europe. Two main thrusts into Manchuria were planned, from the northwest and the east, designed to cut the province in two. Simultaneous attacks (mainly diversionary in nature) were to be made along the Amur river in the north and the Japanese-held islands of Sakhalin and the Kuriles chain off the coast of Siberia. In addition, a mechanized cavalry force would advance across the Gobi Desert towards Peking and seaborne assaults would be made by the Soviet Pacific Fleet along the coast of Korea.

Having declared war on Japan on August 8, Stalin's troops crossed the Manchurian border the following day. It was not the hardest campaign the seasoned Russian troops had ever fought: by August 10 some units were celebrat-

Right: Accurate BDA—bomb damage assessment—in Burma was made difficult owing to the smaller concentration of industries. Strategic and tactical bombing overlapped to a large degree, heavy bombers of Eastern Air Command frequently being asked to hit roads, troops concentrations and individual buildings. Here, Taungup dump area was considered more of a tactical target, and was pattern-bombed by B-24s.

Below: One of the Allied "secret weapons" in the Pacific was underway refueling and replenishment of warships. Freighters transferred thousands of items to fleet units, as in this photo.

Above: Battlefield casualties were transferred to well-equipped hospital ships as quickly as possible, without a potentially dangerous stop in the combat zone.

ing victory, the racing tanks of Marshal Malinovsky's Sixth Guards Tank Army having swept through the Hingan Passes at incredible speed.

Thrown off balance by rapidly unfolding events, Japanese army commanders could not agree to a suitable strategy—there was a desire by some to concentrate on defending Korea— and a counter-attack to cover the line Mukden–Port Arthur was countermanded by Tokyo. Torrential rain and well-fortified Japanese positions halted Marshal Meretskov for about 48 hours, but he then threw in 15 divisions. A spearhead of his First Army took the key town of Mulin, 25 miles east of the frontier. The Japanese fought back bravely, but by the 12th Mutankaing was in Russian hands. Meretskov committed his reserves and with good air support, succeeded in pushing the Japanese westward. To the south the Russian

Twenty-fifth Army stormed positions at Dunnin and prepared to strike from Vladivostok into Korea to link up with a landing by marines of the Pacific Fleet at Seisin and Rasin. The Russians had also taken the southern part of Sakhalin Island before a ceasefire order was issued by Tokyo on August 14. Sporadic fighting continued and, taking advantage of a confused situation, the Russians ranged further afield to secure some significant areas including Port Arthur. The territory secured gave the Russians an opportunity to establish secure military air bases in a remote part of the world, including an early warning radar complex on Sakhalin Island.

THE RECKONING

The economic stranglehold imposed on Japan in 1940–41 prompted the over-confident militarists who held sway over the country to embark on a disastrous war with her Asian neighbors and the Western Allies. It is not just with hindsight that the assessment of the chances Imperial military

Above: The German surrender of May 1945 was as well received in the Pacific as elsewhere.

Left: The fighter director room was arguably the most important area on an escort carrier, an RN vessel being shown here.

forces against the might of the United States can be identified as slim, hamstrung as Japan was by ancient notions of subservience to an Emperor, a figurehead whose voice the vast majority of her soldiers had never even heard let alone seen in the flesh. By following the barbaric and totally outmoded military creed of Bushido, that placed personal sacrifice higher than any prudent need to conserve strength in combat, a foolhardy pride that led to the needless slaughter of thousands of her troops in battles lost before they even started, and a final, incredible self-sacrifice of mass suicide as a national creed, Japan was doomed even as her carrier planes took off for Pearl Harbor on that fateful Sunday in December 1941.

An adversary unlike any other in the 20th century, Japan also followed a policy that fostered pitiless contempt for prisoners of war, a total disregard of civilian casualties, and scant

Above Left: Ratings carry HVAR aircraft rockets across the open deck of a carrier ready to be attached to an attack aircraft.

Left: The most popular announcement over the British Pacific Fleet's loudspeakers was the termination of hostilities with Japan.

Below: Quickly replacing aircraft lost in action was a challenge the BPF met well, especially as some British types could not be replaced from U.S. production. Here a Seafire III is being loaded aboard a carrier.

little heed at the fate of her own population. At the end of the war in which she was internationally condemned as one of the two main aggressors, Japan had given the world a terrifying new word—kamikaze. As her young pilots willingly smashed themselves to death in an often vain effort to sink American warships, the world watched and wondered.

In 1945, Japan's refusal to surrender the most hopeless of lost causes forced the Allies to seek a new, terrifyingly effective way of ending the bloodiest war in history. The threat that kamikaze attacks would turn an invasion of Japan into one of the biggest bloodbaths in history was unacceptable to the Allies—two atomic bombs brought a luckless nation a terrible distinction as the cities of Hiroshima and Nagasaki were obliterated.

Japan's secondary (and poorly publicised) intention of removing the European colonial dominance of Southeast Asia did ultimately bear fruit, but only after Japan had been utterly defeated.

An interesting "alternative history" question is what would have happened had the Japanese attacked only British and Dutch territories in December 1941. Certainly she might have managed to hold onto the territories she had won for longer—and delayed an American entry into the war, perhaps for months. Had the attack on Pearl Harbor not taken place, there would undoubtedly have been a breathing space in the war, but Japan could hardly have ignored the threat on her eastern flank for too long. This all presupposes that the United States would not have declared war the moment the "Pearl of the Orient" was bombed by Japanese aircraft.

Colonial rule had undoubtedly exploited the natural assets of Asian countries for decades and in the immediate postwar years, that rule was reasserted. Spurred by their war support of the Allied cause, Indonesia, India, Pakistan, Indo-China, New Guinea, etc refused to accept the status quo and all ultimately achieved a degree of self rule, with Britain, the Netherlands and France withdrawing. Even the Philippines, with somewhat closer ties to her benefactor state, ceased to be a U.S. possession in 1946.

A less positive, indirect result of Japan's original military expansionism was the adverse reaction to Western influence in those parts of China sympathetic to nationalist rule during the war. Democratic rule along nationalist lines failed to prevail in that vast continent and with the "common enemy" ejected from parts of her territory, China's leaders acted swiftly to "unite" the people under one banner. The move led to the military defeat and retreat of

Below: Royal Navy casevac using a destroyer for maximum speed of transfer for a stretcher case.

nationalist forces to Taiwan and domination of the entire mainland by successive communist regimes.

Japanese occupation of Indo-China proved little short of disastrous at the end of the war. Garrisoned by Japanese troops, fully rearmed courtesy of an overstretched British government, Ho Chi Minh's Viet Minh understandably reacted violently to the return of French colonial rule and declared a republic in 1945. By the time Vietnam erupted into war between the republic and the French, the Japanese troops who had been the unwitting catalysts, had been repatriated. Britain, France, and the Dutch fatally underestimated the degree of national pride in those Asian countries which had thrown in their lot with the Allies to help defeat Japan.

Economically, the Japanese lost all the wartime assets they captured from their eastern neighbors, either through Allied destruction, sabotage, or direct bombing of the factories that so briefly benefited from an influx of raw materials. In the longer term, however, Japan rose like a phoenix from the ashes. From the moral and physical devastation of 1944–45 an economic miracle was wrought by the country's leaders and industrialists (with U.S. cash and cooperation) to a strong economy based on quality consumer goods, automotive products, and, above all, electronics.

Above Left: Bombed at her Kure moorings, the battleship/carrier *Hyuga* was left in no state to continue war operations.

Left: While the main thrust of Operation "Iceberg" saw U.S. forces reduce Okinawa, the British Pacific Fleet operated on the flank, striking Onanagawa Wan and other points to contain enemy reinforcement. Here, a BPF Avenger is photographing the area on August 10, 1945.

Top Right: When Japan finally surrendered, the U.S. fleet staged one of the largest fly-pasts of all time. Thousands of fleet fighters and attack aircraft filled the air over the fleet which rode at anchor off Japan.

Right: Further destruction of the Japanese fleet at Kure captured by U.S. aerial reconnaissance.

While preserving her ancient traditions, Japan turned almost overnight from a nation of belligerent arrogance into a subservient, diligent people, who by application and sheer hard work transformed their devastated land into a world leader—to the point where, despite her precarious position in the politics of the Cold War, she almost totally rejected any form of modern military force to defend herself. Indeed, Southeast Asia Treaty Organization (SEATO) nations grew increasingly frustrated at Japan's intransigent position particularly in the face of Russian naval expansion, and visits to Japanese ports by American nuclear-powered ships were greeted by protests.

However, this "improvement" was accompanied by an internationally condemned reluctance on the part of Japan to objectively come to terms with the past. For years demands for apologies and financial recompense by ex-prisoners of war were ignored by the Japanese leadership, a situation fueled by official visits to countries whose military forces had suffered at Japanese hands.

Toward the end of the 1990s, when such protests gained momentum with even organizations such as the Korean "comfort" women who were forced into prostitution by the Imperial army made their grievances known, Japan finally agreed to make formal apologies and offer a level of financial compensation. Some organiza-

tions, particularly those representing the interests of British PoWs, remain dissatisfied, stating that much more could have been done for more individuals much sooner.

In respect of the Japanese Self Defence Forces, wiser councils eventually prevailed and agreed to a level of modernization, but the defence forces remain of modest size. The ending of the Cold War removed a need for Japan to arm herself further against possible aggression by her old enemy—Russia—but even today Japan remains one of the least militaristic nations of the world.

Right: By the end of the war the Japanese merchant marine had been decimated by Allied anti-ship strikes.

Below: Nagasaki was also carefully combed to determine the unique effects of the A-bomb blast. The demolished chimney stack at right was 1,300ft from ground-zero, the impact point.